Living WITH THE Lectionary

PREACHING THROUGH THE REVISED COMMON LECTIONARY

Living WITH THE Lectionary

PREACHING THROUGH THE REVISED COMMON LECTIONARY

Eugene L. Lowry

ABINGDON PRESS
Nashville

LIVING WITH THE LECTIONARY:
PREACHING THROUGH THE REVISED COMMON LECTIONARY

Copyright © 1992 by Abingdon Press

This book is printed on recycled acid-free paper.

Library of Congress Cataloging-in-Publication Data

LOWRY, EUGENE L.
    Living with the lectionary : preaching through the revised common lectionary / Eugene L. Lowry.
        p. cm.
    ISBN 0-687-17921-1 (alk. paper)
    1. Lectionary preaching. 2. Common lectionary. 3. Bible—Homiletical use. I. Title.
BV4235.L43L69   1992
251—dc20   92-4972
                                                                          CIP

MANUFACTURED IN THE UNITED STATES OF AMERICA

For
my colleagues at
Saint Paul School of Theology

Acknowledgments

I am indebted to many for myriad forms of support and encouragement in the publication of this small volume. I think particularly of the administration and trustees of Saint Paul School of Theology, who made sabbatical time possible for my explorations; my editor, Paul Franklyn, and other officials at Abingdon Press for prompting this writing; and the many pastors who have shared their wisdom and experience. Of course the list is endless—including family and friends. But especially I note the debt I owe to my colleagues at Saint Paul whose support, though less direct in the particulars of the writing, actually has provided the community, the base, the environment in which I have been privileged to work. Without them through all our years together, nothing is even conceivable. Not many have the privilege of working in an academic community which is in fact a community—where one knows and is known in ways that nourish the soul as well as one's field of work. Although we often take it for granted, it is exceedingly rare, and I am grateful.

Contents

Introduction

For years I have experienced a love-hate relationship with the lectionary. In my view the Common Lectionary is both wonderful and terrible—for reasons I will name in the first chapter.

At first I ignored the Common Lectionary, hoping the whole thing might go away, but its growing acceptance in North America in the last fifteen years—particularly where you would least expect it—namely in mainstream, "non-liturgical" Protestantism—suggested that tolerance, perhaps cooperation, maybe even affirmation, might be the wiser stance.

Indeed, in the past fifteen years I would have to acknowledge that the preaching I have heard is substantially better than I heard before, although somewhat more boring. The greatest single variable I am able to detect in this "substantially better" preaching is the increased use of the lectionary as the basis for the sermon.

I know many preachers who share my ambivalence about the lectionary—with some using it unhappily because they know no better way, and some avoiding it while feeling a bit guilty about their nonparticipation.

At one time I decided to publish a one-year optional lectionary so that preachers could jump ship for a while and then return to the A, B, C familiarity. The new Revised Common Lectionary put a halt to those plans. Apparently others were also dissatisfied with some of the sets of readings selected in 1983. As a result, the Consultation on Common Texts commissioned a Task Force on the Common Lectionary to explore widely the Church use of the Common Lectionary and to suggest appropriate changes. The Task Force has finished its work, and Advent 1992 marks the debut of the new Revised Common Lectionary.

Although the new lectionary represents a significant step forward, it is still somewhat problematic for preaching. The purpose of this writing is to name the strengths of lectionary preaching and encourage preachers to be empowered by them, while also naming the weaknesses of lectionary preaching and to suggest ways to avoid the several pitfalls. Chapter 2 will address the question of steps that can be envisioned for otherwise problematic lectionary passages.

It should be noted that nearly all the particular lections discussed in the next chapter have not been changed significantly from the 1983 version of the Common Lectionary. Hence, the primary purpose of this volume in not to critique some new set of problematic passages. It will be to address those lections we have already found difficult to handle. In the process of exploring these passages, certain strategies for handling any and all passages will become evident.

Finally, in chapter 3, "Claims Upon the Preacher," we will explore norms—a kind of homiletical hermeneutic—which might serve as reference points in our preaching task.

Hence, I offer this volume in the hope that lectionary preaching will be empowered. The presenting questions must be, therefore: What are the liabilities and what are the assets of lectionary preaching? Indeed, there are numerous, important assets *and* liabilities of lectionary preaching. First, we will begin with an exploration of the liabilities.

It is my hope that by the time we have concluded our consideration of all the reasons *not* to be a lectionary preacher, many (particularly those who now use the lectionary) will find it difficult to consider ever utilizing it again.

Then we will turn to the assets, and likewise, my hope is that many—particularly those who have never utilized the lectionary for preaching—will find it unthinkable to go another Sunday without it.

Living WITH THE Lectionary

PREACHING THROUGH THE REVISED COMMON LECTIONARY

CHAPTER ONE

Liabilities and Assets of Lectionary Preaching

LIABILITIES

The primary purpose in the development of the various lectionaries has always been to serve liturgical goals (even specifically eucharistic ones) not homiletical objectives. Lectionary rationality is fed by deep biblical and seasonal concerns. In believing that the Church gathers weekly to reenact the drama of salvation, leaders are properly convinced that the sweep of the Christian year must be undergirded at every point by the canon. Paul Bradshaw speaks of this as the anamnetic role of the use of Scripture in worship.[1] This interplay of Scripture and ongoing tradition is not optional for the gathered people of God. Hence, the lectionary serves as biblical grounding for the continuing rhythmic celebration of the acts of God in Jesus Christ.

Moreover, lectionary selections have been based also on a companion role of doxological purpose—that is, the lections are part of the liturgical event of praise. Reading and hearing the lections provide the kind of liturgical orality needed for the proper praise of God. This is all well and good, until one asks if the selected passages will preach. That is, are they the kind of selections which will serve well the homiletical goal of -proclamation? Presently, we will discover that often the answer is no—or at least only with great difficulty.

Indeed, when Horace T. Allen identifies the various functions of lectionary use in the liturgy, *preaching* is only one of the six named (and not the first).[2] Liturgical purposes, not primarily homiletic ones, which lectionary committees attempt to meet by their selection process, result in the functional priority of the synoptic readings—with the other texts serving as co-facilitators (one way or another). The consequence, particularly during the Incarnation/Resurrection cycle of the year, is a kind of thematic unity of the lections.

To be fair here, it ought to be noted that another purpose of the use of Scripture in the liturgy is *didactic* (as Bradshaw identifies it) or *catechetical* (as Allen would call it). Obviously this instructional goal does relate to the preaching office, and historically the homily or sermon would follow immediately upon the reading of the lesson. At the same time, it is a quite narrow view of what preaching is all about. In the Roman Catholic tradition prior to Vatican II, the homily typically was a brief elaboration or explanation of the text—hardly homiletical in shape or purpose.

In short, liturgical interests, particularly doxological and anamnetic have dominated lectionary text selection, and in the process have produced a kind of thematic unity of the lections which does not bode well for the preaching office. We turn now, more specifically, to the various ways this fundamental problem surfaces in lectionary preaching.

Pale Conclusions

One does not need to be an enthusiastic advocate of narrative preaching to recognize that sermons intend to do something, to solve something, to mediate something, to elucidate something. That is, there is an underlying movement intended in whatever shape a sermon takes. Whether one is utilizing a Fosdick method of bringing the wisdom of the ages to bear on a contemporary problem,[3] or with Barth is allowing our considered needs to be thrown up against the veto of the biblical "Nein, wrong question,"[4] the preacher is planning a move *from one reality toward* another. Whether the liberationist preacher is warning one group about God's fundamental freedom in taking sides, or encouraging another group to hold fast to Hope, the sermon attempts to *close a gap*. One may be a narrative preacher who is moving plot-like from opening conflict to final denouement or, following explicitly rhetorical rules, attempting to discern which of three Roman-numeraled points should come first. In whatever case, the movement from before to after, itch to scratch, lost to found, ignorance to discernment is key. "*Once* you were not a people, but *now* you are God's people" (I Peter 2:10, italics mine). Once; now. Once; now. It is basic to the homiletical art. Even with a homiletical moment of corporate celebration, such as a congregational centennial, there is movement from latency to evocation undergirding the preached Word. As Buttrick would have it, the preacher needs to ask: "What is the passage trying to *do*?"[5]—and then behave accordingly, homiletically. Paul Wilson likes to compare the movement of a sermon to dance, "the carefully choreographed, well-rehearsed, artful dance that flows and tumbles like a mountain stream."[6] Preaching is an event-in-time, and fundamentally it is a bridging event, one way or another.

It is not difficult to discern, however, that the doxological/anamnetic/thematic rationale of the lectionary is often achieved by texts of closure. Whether crisp pronouncements of the indicative of the Gospel, salient identification of the Gospel's imperative claim, or faithful witness to the prior acts of God in history, the selections lean heavily toward conclusions. They represent the end of the line of thought. The lectionary makers love *summaries*. Once the text is read, the matter is closed—and often the resultant sermon has the dynamics of a report. Or the preacher is tempted to formulate the summary, explicate it, demonstrate it, illustrate it, amplify it, underline it, elaborate it, and finally—again—to affirm it.

In one sense, this could be justified liturgically. That is, if the liturgy is seen as moving through reenactment of salvific action via eucharist, then this purpose of the lections could be viewed as providing doxological exclamations in the overall process—benchmarks within the action of the liturgy. Those whose liturgical tradition focuses on the Service of the Word, however, do not need a text to slow down the "drama." (In the Roman Catholic traditions which implement the Vatican II conviction that the primary duty of the priest is proclaimer of the Word, the sermons have changed from brief explanations of a text toward fuller homiletical treatment.)

Often it is that when a text veers from simple summation, the pericope will have the several "errant" verses of the text deleted. For example, the passage from Genesis 15 which is chosen includes verses 1-12, and then 17-18 (Year C, Lent 2). Noticing this gap in verses becomes the logical time to explore what got deleted—in this case the unhappy news that Abram's descendants are going to be oppressed for four hundred years. Now, the inclusion of those verses might just provide the homiletical opening we need. Again, Revelation 22 is full of hope, and just what the lectionary planners intend. So, the verses for Year D, Seventh Sunday of Easter are given as 12-14, and then 16-17. Better take a look at verse 15.

Sometimes, the missing verses in the lectionary selection deal not with problematic portions of the text but, rather, with a deletion made for purposes of efficiency. Sometimes such efficiency is counterproductive. For example, in Year C, Fourth Sunday in Lent, the listed gospel lesson is Luke 15:1-3 and 11b-32, which means an introduction and then the prodigal son story. Left out are narratives about the lost sheep and lost coin. Do we need the redundancy? Indeed, we do. Jesus is upsetting the religious crowd by being seen with the wrong people in the wrong places. "This fellow welcomes sinners and eats with them" (15:2). So, Jesus tells three quite different and yet similar stories—which all involve *lost, found,* and *party.* The power comes through shocking redundancy. Without it, one may miss his point altogether. (The missing stories *are* provided at another point in the lectionary process, but in that instance, the prodigal son story is deleted.)

Whatever the tradition, preaching is not enhanced by an overriding commitment to pericope closure. Nor is preaching enabled by constant attempts at thematic unity among the various lections. The overall impact of the lectionary upon preaching may indeed be that of more adequate biblical foundation. But the price has included a tendency to elaborate an unflappable biblical conclusion while missing either the historical context or development of thought, which give summaries to the life of an event. Texts ought to prompt engagement, not call for the benediction.

For example, the first section of Romans utilized in the lectionary after the opening seven-verse salutation is Romans 1:16-17, 3:22*b*-28(29-31) (Year A, Proper 4). This is an extremely important and potentially powerful statement about the good news of the gospel, culminating in verse 24 which announces that all people, Jews and Greek "are now justified by his grace as a gift." (Romans 3:24) The truth is, however, that this culminating announcement grows out of two and a half chapters of argument about the relative merits and failings of both Jews and Greeks. After noting how Greeks may be "inward" Jews, and hence better, he then asks whether being a Jew has any advantage—and answers "Much, in every way" (3:2). At one point he seems to be arguing an ethic of obedience—that God will render judgment according to works (2:6). So, by the time Paul gets to 3:24, and announces the gift, it is a radical reversal from what the previous argument seemed to claim. This crescendo of thought, an ideational narrative, would be explosive in impact, except that these sections are excluded. We receive no surprise, only the final word. Even the two verses utilized from chapter one hide the reality of the argument.

Or again, the Old Testament reading for Year B, First Sunday in Lent is Genesis 9:8-17. This announces God's covenantal relationship with Noah and his descendants. "I have set my bow in the clouds, and it shall be a sign" (9:13). But, the action which leads up to this announcement is missing. Indeed, after the building of the ark and the dynamics of the incredible storm, the rainbow is a bit pale. The judgment on humankind which begins this narrative, and Noah's unique favor with God, are not here. (The building of the ark does occur in Year A, and one can find the rest hidden in the Easter Vigil passages.) As a matter of fact we will miss the drunken episode too. What we have is the rainbow (in a redundant passage).

Obviously the preacher can and ought to move behind the text, finding the lived moment which prompted any given pericope. But when the lectionary selections seem intent on avoiding trouble or issue or problem, or even movement of any kind, the preacher should recognize that the lectionary is making preaching an uphill battle.

Moreover, the quest for thematic and/or seasonal unity among the lections poses additional problems for the lectionary preacher.

Superficial Connections

For one thing, often "thematic unity" turns out to be image or word hopping instead. If a zebra were somehow to show up in the gospel lesson, and perchance there existed a zebra in the Hebrew Scripture, one would likely see the two paired for this particular Sunday. Certainly, the connection of Old and New Testament sheep are well known to lectionary preachers.

One of the worst cases of word hopping or catchword occurs in the texts for Year C, All Saints. The Lukan passage provides the Sermon on the Plain, outlining the radicality of faithful living. The writer to the Ephesians is heard gratefully exclaiming about what can happen when "you may know what is the hope to which he has called you, what are the riches of his glorious inheritance among the saints" (Ephesians 1:18). Then, you notice that the Old Testament lesson comes from Daniel.

What a fine selection of Hebrew Scripture for All Saints. No doubt it will recount how Daniel refused to conform to the country's demand for idolatry, required by King Darius's decree forbidding petition to any one except the king. By being discovered praying next to an open window, Daniel was sent to the den of lions. Perfect for All Saints. No, that is not the passage chosen. Instead, our interest is drawn to Daniel's vision of four beasts coming up out of the sea. But not for long. As soon as the text begins to describe the differences of the beasts, the periocope jumps to Daniel 7:15, which notes Daniel's anxiety regarding the several beasts that were not described for us. But his alarm is quieted by one wise in such matters. He is told the beasts represent four kings. So why was this passage included? Reading the text in the Revised Standard Version at verse 18 (the last verse of the pericope) reveals the answer: "But the saints of the Most High shall receive the kingdom, and possess the kingdom for ever, for ever and ever." *Saints*. There is the connection. Now that the New Revised Standard Version has changed "saints" to "holy ones," we may forever stay in the dark as to why this lection was chosen.

What is worse, we have this passage (and a couple other fairly innocuous ones), but we do not have Nebuchadnezzar's dream or Daniel's interpretation. We do not have the handwriting on the wall or the fiery furnace. We do have the word *saints* (RSV).

Such superficial connections do not provide the continuity that is being claimed. Often in the process the textual integrity of the first lesson is sacrificed on the altar of alleged connection.

In one sense, I am not in a position to object too much about superficial connection since thematic unity of the lections does not run high in my list of priorities. Yet, forcing Old Testament passages to undergird or embellish the gospel lesson, when they have other agenda, is simply neither good theology nor good biblical exegesis.

This issue is exacerbated particularly in the seasons of

Advent and Lent, when the desire to anticipate a salvific act of Christ drags the Hebrew prophets along for a proleptic ride.

Improper Use of Hebrew Scripture

Given the limitation that any selection of passages entails, I think it particularly important to fasten upon the central features of the Old Testament books—particularly less familiar short ones, like Micah and Malachi. As it turns out, in both cases the writers make statements which often have been seen by the church, even the New Testament writers, as anticipating the coming of Jesus. Never mind the overarching purpose of the writing, the contexts which occasioned the writing. When Micah declares: "But you, O Bethlehem of Ephrathah, who are one of the little clans of Judah, from you shall come forth for me one who is to rule in Israel" (5:2), you may be sure that it will be among the two passages cited from the work—even though the lectionary planners had to cut the passage off in mid-sentence at verse 5a in order for it to appear to say what is wanted on the Fourth Sunday in Advent, Year C. Micah's critique of dishonesty in high and low places, his complaint about rich men being full of violence, his sarcasm regarding the one with wicked scales—all these are central to what he was about, and what we ought to be about. His promise of judgment, but final restoration, could be powerful for the pulpits in our time. But such a central passage is not chosen. In particular, where is Micah 4:3: "they shall beat their swords into plowshares, and their spears into pruning hooks"?

Likewise, Malachi's words: "See, I am sending my messenger to prepare the way before me" (3:1) is a favorite for the Advent season—and appears Year C, Second Sunday, but the passage stops one verse before he has a chance to get his message of judgment and justice across. This would be justifiable if sometime within the three-year cycle we could get to the heart of his concern. But it does not happen. His rebuke against "those who oppress the hired workers in their wages, the widow and the orphan, against those who thrust aside the alien, and do not fear me" (vs. 5) is not heard. Indeed, the central motif of the book—a condemnation of priests who corrupt worship by using sick animals for sacrifice, and of teachers who cause many to stumble—is not brought into our time. I think what happens here is a new form of prooftexting, of selectively determining what we find helpful to our Advent cause. Such prooftexting is as surely improper when accomplished through lectionary committee selection as when perpetrated in private sermonic preparation.

Two of the claims of lectionary supporters are that, one, the lectionary covers the canon in a comprehensive way unlikely to happen without it, and two, that as a result lectionary preachers offer a more balanced homiletical fare. In particular, Merrill Abbey once said that "left to our own devices, we necessarily make ourselves at home in the limited arc of the themes that fit our minds. The use of a lectionary, however, 'can stretch our minds to something more approximating the full circle of the gospel.'"[7]

Responded Robert Bolton: "I have no objections if . . . homileticians wish to use a lectionary. And if these preachers want to offer me advice on the task of preparing a balanced diet of preaching, I will listen intently. But . . . how does . . . anyone else know what is the best way for me to preach a balanced Gospel?"[8]

Indeed, it has been observed that the framers of the lectionary have a rather limited arc themselves. So, González and González note that lectionaries "are a selection which reflects the prevailing tradition of the church."[9] In particular, they observe that "Old Testament texts . . . are most often chosen on the basis of their significance for the Christian religion and its observances, rather than on the basis of their significance in showing God's just and loving dealings with the people."[10] More explicitly, "although there are many selections from

Deuteronomy and Leviticus, these have to do mostly with the prescriptions regarding the passover and the shunning of lepers, and nowhere deal with the much more radical views of these two books, that the land belongs to God and cannot be held in perpetuity by anyone, and that at the time of jubilee there shall be a general release from creditors."[11]

One frequently noted limitation of the 1983 Common Lectionary has to do with its woefully inadequate coverage of the role of biblical women. One of the most helpful changes in the 1992 Revised Common Lectionary is the commitment to remedy this situation. As a result, the new lectionary includes narratives about Sarah, Hagar, Rebekah, Leah, Miriam, Deborah, Lydia, the woman with the issue of blood, the Syrophoenician woman, the good woman of Proverbs 31, and Hannah. None of these was utilized in the previous set of lections.

Sermon Series Limitation

Use of the lectionary in preaching closes the door on many forms of sermon series preaching. Although the lectionary's commitment to the Christian year is helpful for series preaching, particularly in Advent and Lent, and certainly during the ordinary cycle by means of its following the Gospels chapter by chapter, other sermon series forms tend to be cut out. For example, the lectionary will not provide a sequence for the parables of Jesus, nor passages for an ongoing season of doctrinal/credo sermons. Nor will it give the preacher a set of Old Testament passages by which to do a sermon series, for example, on the minor prophets. Nor is it probable that a pastor can devise a missional sermon series to follow the Day of Pentecost and still follow the lectionary. During the ordinary cycle of the year, the Revised Common Lectionary will, however, provide a sequence from the Mosaic tradition in Year A, a David sequence in Year B, and major prophets in Year C.

This issue emerges, not because of any restricted comprehensiveness of the lectionary as such, but rather because of the organizing mentality of the lectionary. In short, the joint commitment to the seasons and to thematic unity—together with separation of the synoptic Gospels into Years A, B, and C—mitigates against some forms of sermon series which can be quite enriching for the local congregation.

Quick Fix Lectionary Aids

Finally, there is another emergent problem for lectionary preaching that consists not of some inherent lectionary weakness, per se, but rather surfaces as a tempting tendency among lectionary preachers.

With so many preachers utilizing the lectionary, there arises naturally a substantial body of published preaching aid material which when utilized improperly can stifle powerful preaching. I refer to the several biblical resource pieces which follow the lectionary sequence. Some of this material is quite good—indeed, coming from the pens of noteworthy scholars and powerful preachers.

The problem is that lectionary preachers often turn to these helpful aids prior to having internalized the texts. When I have inquired of lectionary preachers, how they prepare—the sequence of their work—I find a trend. Often, they read the text and immediately turn to the published lectionary commentaries. They may receive good advice, but altogether prematurely. In short, at the point in sermon preparation when they ought to be internalizing the text and exploring the many questions which might emerge, they are already finding answers to the questions they have not yet raised. The result is a homiletical preparation short-circuit. As Fred Craddock explains: "When used at the proper time they are indispensable, but if too early opened, they take over. They suppress and intimidate the preacher. After all, who is going to venture a thought or an interpretation when at the very same desk are six internationally known Bible scholars?''[12]

Then again, there is one particularly problematic lectionary "aid"—namely the Lectionary Bible, which includes only the verses which are included in the lessons for Sunday. Without proper reflection about what is happening, the canon suddenly shrinks markedly. With the doxological/thematic mentality of the lectionary, one might never know what is missing.

But, is it not true that non-lectionary preachers also face the temptation of seeking answers before asking crucial questions? Of course, but for some reason I have not found it to be as prevalent. Perhaps this is so because of a difference of mentality I perceive to exist between lectionary and non-lectionary preachers. I have found a style that often leads to not asking the hard questions because of a flow from 1) a given text to 2) proper expert advice to 3) homiletical application. Non-lectionary preachers are more likely to have a different but prevalent temptation, which flows from 1) pastoral issue to 2) relevant text to 3) homiletical advice.

ASSETS

Having explored several liabilities of utilizing the Revised Common Lectionary in preaching, what about advantages? What are the assets of lectionary preaching? We might be assisted by naming the strengths it offers.

Comprehensive Planning

The most immediately obvious advantage of lectionary preaching is that it provides a thoughtful and well-established comprehensive plan for our preaching. Almost all the preachers with whom I have visited on this subject say there is nothing so chronically worrisome about the preaching office than to wonder "well, what now?" I can recall my early days in preaching, of spending enormous amounts of time, not simply in preparing Sunday's sermon but in wondering what theme the sermon might address. Then I also would have to ask: Where do I start this time—with a text, a pastoral experience, some world event—perhaps a recently read book? Sometimes I would begin reading a book, hoping some light bulb would go on. If one did, then I would have to explore when last some similar bulb lit up.

It did finally dawn on me that I needed a long-term plan. I did not then know anything about lectionaries (this was long before the common lectionary emerged). I did find the book by Andrew Blackwood on *Planning a Year's Pulpit Work,*[13] which followed the Christian year—together with what I would call a "cultural season year"—but did not recommend specific texts for each Sunday. It named the fall of the year as a time for preaching from the Old Testament, Christmas to Easter for preaching around the life and ministry of Christ, post-Easter sermons focused on the church, and then, finally, addressing the question of ministry in the world—until it was time for the Old Testament again. It espoused much use of sermon series. Each summer I would take one week to devise next year's fare.

Indeed, there are those now who would offer similar plans to that of Blackwood. Would such a plan be equally effective? Yes and no. Yes, it is a systematic plan enabling one to not scramble each week, wondering what next to do. No, in that it adds to the potential liability of the lectionary sequences by making the individual preacher the controller of the sequence. All of which means that I am left to my own leanings, perhaps uncritically. If I am a life-situation preacher, the pulpit fare will be addressing many issues, probably with less attention to a comprehensive biblical plan. If I am a bible student at heart, the congregation may not feel heard, and hence not significantly addressed. Perhaps this rationale may appear a bit contrived, even reductionistic, but the point is: If I devise the plan, it is difficult to be brought up against norms beyond my own leanings. The preacher may be critical of the common lectionary precisely because there is a tension between personal canons and canons selected by the community. The problem with our own mentality is that we do not so easily notice it—let alone successfully resolve the limitations it provides.

Even though these personal/professional leanings can and will also alter the way a preacher utilizes the lectionary, there is still a reference-point outside oneself, even pushing against natural leanings. Moreover, the resources available "around" the lectionary cannot be found for a personally devised system. It is nearly impossible, economically and physically, for any preacher to amass such materials in any other way.

Likewise, preaching without the Common Lectionary is to set aside the comprehensive biblical base that many scholars have invested incredible amounts of expertise and time to produce. And the result is something *given,* not *chosen,* which almost certainly will stretch the canonical parameters of any preacher.

There are two factors in this assessment. First, we all have our favorite texts, those portions of scripture which blend nicely into our thinking. They are home for us—our personal canon within the canon. Because they represent the very heart of what we take the gospel to be, it is almost impossible to stay away from them. Moreover, because they are so internalized into the fabric of our being, there are few surprises for us in them anymore. Indeed, there are probably few surprises for our listeners too.

But there is a deeper more insidious temptation lurking here. Without the influence of outside pericope planning, the preacher often leans toward a topical preaching program. So I decide to preach *on* this subject, and the following Sunday *on* that subject. I am tempted to move from the pastoral issue to relevant text to homiletical advice. The problem is related both to *control* and *direct focus*. Lost is the kind of indirection Craddock spoke about in *Overhearing the Gospel*. It is not simply that parishioners receive a weekly frontal attack on an issue; it is first of all, that the preacher's own selective preparation process tends to preclude any overhearing in the sermon preparation process. "Have you not gone to the Scriptures," asked Craddock, "demanding that they speak *directly* to you . . . and, in reflection later, had to admit to assault and rape of the text?"[14] On the other hand, "on other occasions, the distance provided by the anonymity of the writer, the alien time and place of the narrative, and the general feeling of 'this is for someone else,' dropped defenses, removed the threat that closes eye and ear, set you free, and hence permitted the Word to come to you."[15] This is precisely the difference between the text hunting process "on the make" and the sometimes wonderfully out-of-step, and obviously-meant-for-someone-else, text that the lectionary provides. It is, as Craddock explains, that "distance tends to increase involvement because without distance, involvement is too aware of self."[16] Wilson notes that like electricity "the spark of imagination happens when two ideas that seem to have no apparent connection . . . are brought together." But, not too closely together. "Touching wires [have] no visible spark."[17]

Sometimes the kind of sermon series that I noted earlier to be difficult with lectionary preaching can help alleviate this problem. For example, if one were to decide to preach a series of sermons on the minor prophets, deciding early on only the names of those prophets to be covered, then it is possible to be surprised by what one might find during the explicit exploration of the text. All of which leads us to what I consider a primary problem for non-lectionary preachers. I call it serendipitous juxtaposition.

Serendipitous Juxtaposition

Not only is it true that the lectionary provides preachers with texts they otherwise wouldn't touch with a ten-foot pole—and hence surprise is possible—it is also true that the lectionary planners have no way to know what significant events might occur in the congregation or the wider world. What might seem a decided disadvantage—namely that the pericopes are not "timely" in this sense—often becomes powerfully timely by bridging the biblical and contemporary world in serendipitous fashion. For example, when the conflict in the Persian Gulf struck the world, non-lectionary preachers were hunting their favorite texts (whatever their position on the war). Meanwhile, lectionary preachers were assessing the given lections to discern if that world and this world really connect. All of which opens the door to possible serendipity, homiletically—even spiritually. Is it not the case that often the text that seemed most impossible evoked a remarkably powerful sermon, while the easy to apply text helped the sermon to fall flat? The connections were too obvious both for preacher and congregation.

Collaborative Possibilities

Another asset which is often overlooked by those considering assets and liabilities of lectionary preaching is that of collaborative work of several kinds.

Dr. Gilbert Ferrell has spent many years with lectionary preaching in United Methodist churches in Texas. He testifies that his lectionary study groups, which always meet on Sunday evenings, have literally transformed the life of the congregation. Note that 1) this study comes early in the week, and 2) their work is intended to start a process, not finish it. That is, the agenda is not to prepare next Sunday's sermon. Rather, it is to explore the text with Dr. Ferrell. There are two main results. First, the preacher's imagintion is whetted by the diversity of outlook always present in the group, and second, the group brings an entirely different set of expectations to the sermon event next Sunday. Their investment in the scripture evokes a readiness to hear the Word. The study group has literally taught them how to listen. And this is not limited to the specific texts that they have explored together. As parishioners rotate out of the group in order to allow others in, the former participants discover that they continue to be present for the sermon in a qualitatively different way than ever before. The mentality of speaker to audience simply cannot survive this corporate experience, and becomes transformed into an eagerly listening people of God.

Likewise, the possible corporate learning experience of clergy can have a similar effect. I have often been told of small town or county ministerial alliances which were near death because of lowest common denominator relationships which came alive when the ministers gathered on Monday morning to explore the sacred texts. Even clergy who do not follow the lectionary in their preaching find it an important event of the week. It was surprising, they report, how much we actually have in common. The diversities became enriching rather than divisive, and again the individual preachers would be simulated toward Sunday's sermon.

Ecclesiological Symbol

At a deeper level yet, and even more basic than the collaborative possibilities, lectionary use participates as an ecclesiological symbol. It not only names but participate in the corporate nature of the church. There is a remarkable difference between recognition that "these are the church's texts for today"—with people aware that were they to go down the street to another worshiping congregation that still "these are the church's texts for today"—and people coming to church wondering "what has the pastor been thinking about this week?" Participation in the common lectionary helps the church avoid the Lone-Ranger pulpit mentality. Mind you, we are not just discussing actual words or named reactions, as much as that unnamed reality whose power is in part its unconscious dimension.

For example, I once read someone's distinction between Catholic and Protestant worship as consisting in the fact that "Catholic worship lights a candle on the altar for God to see while Protestant worship places flowers on the table for the people to see." I doubt whether the average Catholic or Protestant worshiper could articulate such a truth, but I believe most can sense the reality to which the words refer. So it is, I believe, that the very fact of a *Common* Lectionary has powerful significance in the life of the church—and mitigates against the entrepreneurial nature of the sermonic "main event."

I recall serving with a pastor who memorized the entire funeral service. He never needed the little black book. Folks were always impressed. Yet there was something unsettling about it for me that I could not name—that is, until after I had read and finally understood Tillich's treatment of symbol in *Dynamics of Faith*.[18] The little black book, particularly in the context of a secular funeral home, brought the Church in with the preacher. Except this preacher didn't. It made a significant difference. So it is that corporate events such as participation in the common lectionary produce a powerful symbolic difference in the life of the gathered chrch.

Integration of Sermon and Liturgy

Perhaps in part a consequence of such symbolic realities, congregations utilizing the Common Lectionary appear to have greater integrity of sermon and liturgy. More particularly, there is more use of Scripture in lectionary congregations. I mean this in a larger sense than the simple fact of multiple passages being read during the service. Prayers, litanies, and other acts of praise appear to have a decidedly greater biblical cast. Altogether, I am suggesting that the use of the Common Lectionary enhances the lived sense of canonical inclusion in the tradition. Indeed, I recommend use of the lectionary in the service even if the preacher goes another route.

At the level of liturgical practicality, use of the Common Lectionary, and hence faithful attention to the Christian year, enables greater anticipation and, as a result, more effective participation by other worship leaders in the congregation. People know how to coordinate their efforts into the rhythmic sweep of the liturgical year. The texts assist in experiencing the whole gospel each Sunday.

And yet, a word of caution is needed here—at least for those of us in non high-church middle Protestantism. We tend to thematize altogether too much. So the text calls for a sermon on forgiveness. The word goes out to the choir director, who obliges with an anthem on forgiveness. By Sunday the hymns are forgiving—and so everything else. Trouble is, forgiveness is only a part of what is adequate for any experience of Sunday worship. The people of God need the whole gospel every Sunday, not forgiveness this Sunday, justice next Sunday, and confession the next. Indeed, this concern underlies my reservation about the Revised Common Lectionary's thematic mentality—united as it is around the gospel lesson. Certainly, we need liturgical cohesiveness; we also need the contrast of juxtaposition. Having granted this concern, it is nonetheless true, I believe, that utlilization of the common lectionary reinforces the corporate nature of the Church.

Biblical Mentality

Finally, taking matters a step further, the result of lectionary use for the church at large, as well as for the individual congregation, is the development of a biblical mentality within the church.

For too long, and perhaps growing out of the modernist/ fundamentalist controversy in the 1920s, mainstream Protestantism has found itself in a strange position. Unlike the Roman

Catholic, Orthodox, Episcopal, and even Lutheran traditions which have understood the Service of the Table as the central liturgical focus, middle Protestantism has focused on the Service of the Word, presumably centered on the Bible. But given the rise of biblical higher criticism in the nineteenth century, it could no longer thump the pulpit with biblical prooftexts—as fundamentalist churches did. Its growing dis-ease with difficult to understand and, perhaps to some, embarrassing passages resulted in the Bible's removal to the side of the podium for the sake of the newer focus of topical address. Biblical expository preaching got replaced with thematic life-situation sermons which had a biblical text to be sure, but often not a generative one which could serve as the core of the sermon. The core of the sermon more likely was a salient idea, a relevant theme—like love, or stewardship, or service. The Bible became a resource, and the preacher could pick a brief text with care (one that didn't have any problem features like fishes swallowing people).

The Random House Dictionary defines the term *resource,* to mean some "support or aid," particularly one "held in reserve," to which one may turn "in an emergency."[19] That sums it up quite nicely. What was true for the pulpit was at the time becoming the modus operandi for the Sunday School (I mean, of course, the Church School), and for the Vacation Bible School (that is, Vacation Church School). The advance in educational philosophy in North America was emerging in the lesson plans for Sunday. Memorizing verses in the Bible fell otu of favor for the sake of more utilitarian educational enterprises. The notion of the Bible as *source* (defined by the dictionary as "origin . . .[or] to spring up")[20] became the property of the "unenlightened" right wing of Protestantism.

Increasingly, the "princes of the pulpit" became other than the Fosdick*s* and David H.C. Read*s*, for whom the Bible was central to their very beings. Those with the gifts of anecdote and psychological sensibilities became the models for the Protestant pulpit. Though certainly not in theory, yet in practice the Bible increasingly became peripheral.

But the emergence of lectionary use in preaching now signals a new direction in the life of the church. One ought not claim that lectionary use is the sole cause of this shift. But its use is certainly more than a reflection of the mood of the church. When three or four passages are always shaping the liturgy for the morning, we observe a re-imaging of what it means to be the people of God. Indeed, the very fact that the lections are given, not chosen, is a powerful symbol that the church is something other than a voluntary association of like-minded people. We are engrafted. The church is a gift of God, established by Christ, not a bunch of individuals who get together for a commonly-decided purpose. The cycle of the Christian year and the "givens" of the lectionary in worship signal the community as other than some kind of private entrepreneurship. And the Bible is recognized as the centerpiece of the covenant community. Little wonder that in almost every denomination there has emerged some kind of significant long-term, in-depth Bible study program.

In short, lectionary use bespeaks a new centering, a new mentality in the life of the church—and the Bible is at the core, not as *resource* but as *source*. Utilization of the Revised Common Lectionary for preaching provides both formidable problems and substantial advantages. The question which naturally emerges is how to reap the advantages of lectionary use, and how to avoid the liabilities.

CHAPTER TWO

Overcoming the Obstacles of Lectionary Preaching

The question before us, then, is how to most effectively participate in lectionary preaching without falling into the several traps encouraged by the lectionary.

In this chapter we explore specific lections that are in the new Revised Common Lectionary, and which I believe are problematic for preachers. In the process of discussing these texts for specific possible homiletical use, we will be naming the problems and discovering potential remedies.

Before turning to the first text, we recall briefly the dominant principle which, in my view, underlies sermonic work. We recall several words or phrases already used repeatedly. For example, a sermon can be conceptualized by the term *bridging* (as a verb) or a *bridging event* (as a noun). The purpose of any sermon is always to *close a gap*. The juxtaposition of *once, now,* is central, regardless of the "type" of sermon. A sermon seeks to *do* something.

Recall Paul Wilson's notion of the electrical arc, which he discovered in a high school physics class. A student would crank an old farmhouse telephone generator while the teacher "brought the ends of the two wires closer and closer together." As he reports it: "When the ends were six inches apart, a spark jumped through the air with a snap. When the ends were four inches apart there was a crackling sound and a waving but constant spark between the two ends."[1]

Suppose we imagine any sermon to happen when the wires are between four and six inches apart. But what wires? I propose that we think of the sermonic *issue* as one (negative) pole and the sermonic *resolution* as the other (positive) pole. In the actual sermon, such matters become more complicated than this image suggests, but for now the image of electrical poles alerts us to a fundamental consideration in sermon preparation. As an alternative to the predictability of electrical arcs, it could be said that we are seeking a human connection between some kind of "itch" and some kind of "scratch."

One of the first critical tasks of sermon preparation, then, is to identify what the two poles are. This identification will not be "set in concrete," but at least conceptually imaged. I have already complained that the lectionary tends to hand the preacher an answer—the positive pole. If that be true in a given text, the preacher's next move is to look for the other wire, which, indeed, may only be implied in a text. Sometimes it is, in fact, absent entirely, and we may need to do some historical-critical work to find the issues. Sometimes that other wire exists in the life of the congregation which will be receiving the sermon. On some rare occasions, the biblical text will provide the negative pole, and we will begin hunting for the other one. Sometimes the text may actually provide both ends, positive and negative. Even more rarely, a text will be the electrical arc spanning both wires. The point is to *name* what we have been given so we can know how to proceed.

Obviously, our naming of the poles presumes that we have already allowed ourselves to be thoroughly charged with the text in question—which is not likely to occur by a quick cursory reading. This preliminary process is discussed as saturation in a previous writing, *How to Preach a Parable*.[2]

Given the lectionary's penchant for summaries, for resolution, chances are very great that our first critical work will be to look for trouble, to expose the negative pole. (We can work on cranking generators and perceiving electrical arcs later.) The key consideration here is to understand that the sense of perceived juxtaposition is what births effective sermon preparation.

So, therefore, with this preliminary principle in mind regarding initial sermon preparation work, we explore some texts. In our consideration, we need to remember that all of these texts were given by previous lectionary committees—not the present revision committee. It too inherited them. I will make note of those instances when revision is involved.

The Case of the Pale Middle

*Jonah 3:1-5, 10 (**Year B, 3rd Sunday After Epiphany**)*

The text could not be more positive. Another term might be *bland*. In its worst sense, the text is a violation of the book as a whole. Every story, we are told, has a beginning, a middle, and an ending. Not our pericope, here. We have the pale middle, only. Why we are given no more of the tale is difficult to discern. Can Jonah's eventual trip to Nineveh be properly understood without reference to his initial dramatic rebellion? Surely not. Obviously one cannot read the entire book on a given Sunday, but why are these particular verses the chosen ones? Perhaps the text was a nice "fit" for the gospel (Mark 1:14-20) in which "Jesus came to Galilee, proclaiming the good news of God" and declaring "the time is fulfilled" (1:14-15). Here Jonah is instructed to "Get up, go to Nineveh, that great city, and proclaim to it the message" (3:2). But, if so, such quick connection becomes false witness—unless one is prepared to imagine that Jesus went reluctantly to Galilee.

The problem is not just that we miss Jonah's bad attitude toward the Ninevites (which has interesting homiletical potential for the question of evangelism in any age), but we miss out on that incredible theological moment when Jonah can be caught in midair between the certainty of judgment (aboard ship) and the miracle of grace (in the deep.) Even before that dramatic moment, Jonah is on the run from God—having an equally narrow-minded notion about God's jurisdiction.

The apparently happy ending to his evangelistic endeavors is not the story's actual conclusion. Just one verse later, we might have heard the awful truth that "this was very displeasing to Jonah, and he became angry" (4:1). How could anybody so attuned to the voice of God find fault with God's acts of mercy? Well, because he knew that God was wrong, of course. (More potential homiletical arcs of electrical change.) But, not included. We have the pale middle, which when utilized alone violates the entire book. It should be noted that groups who follow the alternate Old Testament lessons for the Sundays after Pentecost, Year A (namely, the Roman Catholics, Lutherans, and Episcopalians) will find the fourth chapter listed for Proper 20. The rest of us have only these six verses in chapter three. (And in that other case of alternate readings, the text begins with God's repentance, without knowing what the repentance is all about.)

Before considering how to handle this lection, we might observe a lesser yet significant additional problem to the text as provided by the lectionary.

Given the small slice of the book of Jonah included, it is remarkable that even this brief section is chopped. We are given 3:1-5, 10. What happened to verses 6 through 9? With such a short passage, why make it even shorter? One can only conjecture the motivation. It is, of course, possible that some readers may see a redundancy here, namely that verse 5 in a matter of fact manner notes that a fast was being observed ". . . and everyone great and small put on a sackcloth." Verse 7 details the king's proclamation of a fast. If this is an untoward duplication, then if necessary the second and more detailed description as told in verses 6 through 9 should be retained, while dropping verse 5. Whatever the case, verses 6 through 9 are important for the following reason.

Remembering Craddock's observation about the fact that people resent arriving at the destination of a trip they have not taken,[3] we should attend to the movement that verses 6 through 9 articulate. "When the news reached the king . . . he rose . . . removed his robe, covered himself with sackcloth, and sat in ashes'' (3:6). Immediately, "he had a proclamation made'' (3:7a), and then the text gives the proclamation verbatim (verses 7b-9). Even the animals were prohibited from food and drink. The king is moved toward hope: "Who knows? God may relent and change his mind; he may turn from his fierce anger, so that we do not perish.'' (verse 9) Notice the crescendo of action and thought which leads to the marvelous climax of verse ten that "When God saw . . . how they turned from their evil ways, God changed his mind . . . and he did not do it.'' Wow!

Yes, but some may say, the key is simply the fact that God did not do it. That's the bottom line, and it is given in the pericope, so what is the complaint? But verse 10 is not simply the bottom line, it is the punch line of the sequence. When you delete the sequence, you pull the punch.

When the king says "who knows,'' the electric wires are being brought together, and with God's response in verse ten, the arc happens—you can see the light, hear the buzzing, feel the tingle. I suspect that proper closure was desired for this text. The connection to the synoptic passage regarding "proclaiming . . . the message'' may be all that triggered the inclusion of Jonah in three versions of the Christian year. Pity.

But now to the larger issue. What does the preacher do to faithfully preach from the book of Jonah? One main decision has to do with how many sermons are going to be generated from the text. For example, there is a whole sermon that can be derived from just that part of chapter one in which the sailors representing numerous religions all are converted. They are converted—even in the context of Jonah's rebellion. Another potential sermon is apparent in the consideration of Jonah's motive for boarding the ship bound for Tarshish, thinking he can get outside earshot of Yahweh.

But let us presume that to stay in step with the lectionary, we are to prepare only one sermon from the book of Jonah for this three-year cycle. What do we need to do?

First, in order to be true to the integrity of the book, we must find a way to cover the sweep of all four chapters, even though we will focus sharply at probably only one point. Note, that it will not do simply to drag in every verse, as if equidistant from every other. There is simply too much here. So, we will intend to make sure the context and overall sweep of action is briefly covered while lingering long enough to engage the central focus. But what is the focus? That, of course, will depend on what we intend the sermon to do. We must imagine the basic issue that is at stake in the text, which likewise will become the basic issue of the sermon as preached.

One might think of this step as naming the negative pole. It is very important to do this in some depth and clarity before naming precisely the positive pole. In such powerful biblical stories as this one, however, it is often difficult to delay the positive naming because the story presents everything so crisply. But, note the point here—that if the sermon preparer moves too quickly to the resolution of things, often a premature and sometimes superficial arc is produced which has little power.

What might qualify as a basic issue presented here? Although interrelated, we can separate several for starters. For example, Jonah's narrow mindedness about the Ninevites. This is surely central. Jonah's rush to get away from God's word might be another. One might consider what lies behind the fact that everybody repents here, except Jonah. The sailors repent, the Ninevites repent, God repents. In fact, in the sense of "turning around" even the fish repents by vomiting out Jonah. Jonah does *not* repent. Indeed, one might expect some sign of repentance in his prayer from inside the fish, but he delivers a psalm of thanksgiving instead. Very revealing. One could imagine a sermon which comes altogether from inside the fish—with flash backs and flash forwards. As another dominant issue one's work might focus on why God would even call someone as stubborn as Jonah.

Whatever the focus, it should provide an issue which is true to the text, generative in shaping the necessary juxtaposition, and faithful in finally evoking the word of God for the congregation. But to do this, I believe it essential, one way or another, to treat the entirety of the book's thrust. Clearly, the text involved must be more than 3:1-5, 10.

When Carefulness Goes Too Far

Galatians 1:1-12	**(Year C, 2nd Sunday After Pentecost, Proper 4)**
Galatians 1:11-24	**(Year C, 3rd A P, Proper 5)**
Galatians 2:15-21	**(Year C, 4th A P, Proper 6)**
Galatians 3:23-29	**(Year C, 5th A P, Proper 7**
Galatians 5:1, 13-25	**(Year C, 6th A P, Proper 8)**
Galatians 6:(1-6) 7-16	**(Year C, 7th A P, Proper 9)**

In Year C of the lectionary immediately following Trinity Sunday, there are six weeks in succession which provide a wonderful opportunity to preach from the book of Galatians (the period from approximately May 9th through July 9th). As the Oxford Annotated Bible puts it in its introduction: "Often called the Magna Charta of Christian liberty, the Letter to the Galatians deals with the question whether a Gentile must become a Jew before he can become a Christian."[4] Moreover, because the occasion for its writing is a time of intense conflict, Paul's theologizing is particularly fervent and articulate—if occasionally awkward. His red-faced passion makes his message potent, if sometimes crude.

Our present exploration of these texts gains focus not simply upon significant problems regarding lectionary selection, but also from the fact that the granting of six Sundays' sermon time (theoretically) is particularly rich in potential. We can be grateful to those who granted us so much opportunity with these powerful six chapters. It is easy to imagine how a preacher might craft a sermon series that could address crucial theological and historical issues such as the doctrine of justification, the Christian's relation to the Mosaic law, the nature of Christian freedom, or growth in discipleship.

The lectionary preacher must be cautious, however, because the passages as selected tend to blur the specifics of the conflict going on in Galatia while zooming in crisply for the resultant doctrinal affirmations.

The selection process begins well with the first two pericopes (Galatians 1:1-12 and Galatians 1:11-24) providing Paul's open foray. He registers his utter amazement at their "so quickly deserting the one who called you in the grace of Christ" (1:6). Note, too, that Paul has no opening words of commendation and thanksgiving that we have come to expect. By implication in the very first passage he names the charges others have brought against him—namely, that he is a second-rate apostle, he takes the orders from Jerusalem, and he is a crowd pleaser. So far so good. But note what happens in the subsequent lections.

Especially important is that in Galatians 2:1-19 the argument escalates significantly, but not in our selections. Central to the building of tension, and probably the most dramatic vignettes in the entire letter is his stinging rebuke of Cephas, recounted for the Galatians. Regrettably, it is not here. "Even Barnabas was led astray by their hypocrisy" (2:13), Paul laments. But the contemporary congregation will not heard it read.

Note that the lection for this Sunday is Galatians 2:15-21, which begins *immediately after* Paul's rebuke. Note, too, that verses 15-18 complete an argument *not disclosed*. Indeed, the lectionary picks up as he is ready to settle down: "I have been crucified with Christ; and it is no longer I who live, but it is Christ who lives in me" (verse 20). It is a crisp sentence to be sure, but the affirmation becomes bland without the previous passionate encounter.

Unfortunately, the current lectionary also excludes his calling the Galatians stupid (as translated by the New English Bible) and deletes his powerful use of rhetorical questioning: "Did you receive the Spirit by doing the works of the law or by believing what you heard? Are you so foolish? Having started with the Spirit, are you now ending with the flesh? Did you experience so much for nothing?" (Galatians 3:2b-4a). All this is missing in the revision.

But let us look back again at the omission of the Cephas rebuke, and assess its impact for our preaching. It is one thing for Paul to rail against the Judaizers who followed him into the region of Galatia. No names; no faces. They have a straw-like character. It is quite another thing for all to know that it is Cephas who is the foe here, and with him the Jerusalem church—"supposed to be acknowledged leaders (what they actually were makes no difference to me)" (2:6). Well, this is heady conflict, if only we were privy both to the experience in Antioch and the account of his journeys to Jerusalem. We have neither.

We have here a full-fledged, in-house, family argument among those we know by name. "If you, though a Jew, live like a Gentile, and not like a Jew, how can you compel the Gentiles to live like Jews?" (2:14). Take that, Cephas! But when this section is missing, the focus of conflict is blurred, the opponents scarcely known. And his victory statement shrinks to pale affirmation: "I do not nullify the grace of God: for if justification comes through the law, then Christ died for nothing" (2:21).

The next lectionary passage comes after Paul cools down enough to say something positive about the law as custodian. At the same time—and with fairness—it ought to be noted that the lectionary does include the marvelous passage about having put on Christ through baptism, and hence "There is no longer Jew or Greek, there is no longer slave nor free" (3:28).

Chapter Four—omitted in these six pericopes—is a most remarkable passage in that Paul's previous positive relationship to the Galatians is fondly remembered, and we find a virtual roller-coaster ride of emotions from burning anger to intimate lament. One wonders if it were Paul's recollection of God having "sent the Spirit of his Son into our hearts, crying 'Abba! Father!'" (4:6) that prompted him to ask: "What has become of the good will you felt?"—why, "you would have torn out your eyes and given them to me" (4:15), and finally to personal regret: "I wish I were present with you now and could change my tone, for I am perplexed about you" (4:20). What remarkably intimate tough love.

All this is excluded from the lectionary texts, which skip to the charge, "For freedom Christ has set us free. Stand firm, therefore, and do not submit again to a yoke of slavery" (5:1).

The problem continues. The roller coaster of argument and emotion is about to provide the final thrill of juxtaposition, but we will receive only the level-plane second half of it.

Note that the next pericope is Galatians 5:1, 13-25. We just noted, above, his declaration about freedom (verse 1), and verses 13-25 will delineate his summons to not "use your freedom as an opportunity for self-indulgence" (5:13). But what happens in verses 2 through 12? It is his concluding tour de force against his opponents who have "prevented you from obeying the truth" (5:7). Linking his cause with the Lord against those who inevitably will face judgment for their espousal of circumcision, he blurts out his rage: "I wish those who unsettle you would castrate themselves!" (5:12). It is in the context of this verbal explosion against returning to the law that Paul surely anticipates a possible unwanted consequence which he needs immediately to counter—namely that of license. Quickly he warns "Only do not use your freedom as an opportunity for self-indulgence" (5:13). Moreover, "live by the Spirit'' (5:16). One can feel the verbal power of juxtaposition—from angry explosion in the context of freedom to resultant admonition regarding discipline. Without the first half, the second becomes mere advice.

Abundantly clear in all of this is that preachers are charged with faithfulness both to the *purpose* of the text—asking what does the text intend to do—and to the *form* the text takes. The lectionary selections from Galatians do not inflect gross damage to the integrity of the letter as such. This is entirely different from the problem presented by the Jonah selection. The narrative shape of the letter, however, is badly mutilated. And we need to remember that shape and purpose are not unrelated entities. As David Bartlett puts it: ''Questions of form are not separable from questions of content.''[5] Hence, ''we cannot be faithful to the text . . . without attending to the history behind the text''[6]—and it should be added here, even the angry state of mind of Paul unmistakably revealed in the text.

Frankly, what gets included and excluded gives the appearance of too much ''carefulness,'' coupled with a leaning toward affirmational closure. Three kinds of passages tend to be excluded in the readings from Galatians, ones with sharp edges of anger, ones with complication of argument, and ones with explicit dialogical conflict. It is as though the choosers often waited for the purple passages of articulate resolution. The preacher should *reintroduce* the fullness of conflict and remember the principle of juxtaposition. Then the purple passages can burst forth with power.

There are some preachers whose particular communions do not encourage (or allow) redrafting of the passages to be read in the service. For others, changing a pericope is a viable option. In either case, the sermon itself can range wherever the preacher desires. When the passage excludes a vital preface to its meaning or a necessary prior act in its drama, the preacher can easily suspend the flow of the preached lection at precisely the point when the previous material is needed for meaning and for power.

One very easy technique is simply to call the congregation's attention to what appears to be a disconnected affirmation. For example: "Paul's admonition here to stand fast in the freedom of Christ seems true enough, and obvious enough—until you begin to ask, well, what might get in its way? Well . . ." Or again: "You know, when Paul says in verse 11 that the gospel he preached 'is not of human origin; for I did not receive it from a human source' (1:11), I'm inclined to respond, well of course, we all know that . . . But then I realize this is the second time in eleven verses he has said that. Right at the first he said 'Paul, an apostle, sent neither by human commission nor from human authorities' (1:1). And you begin to wonder, why is he making such a point of this anyway?"

Please note the difference between these two simple examples of suspension and the "facts first" method with which I was raised. In my childhood, I grew accustomed to an expository style of preaching which settled everything first, before the sermon could get off the ground. Compare: "Our text today begins with Paul's confidence in his own divine calling. With this assurance he helps explain to the Galatians the very nature of the freedom Christ offers." No juxtaposition in that rendering—only closure. Whatever sections, issues, and themes become the substance of one's preaching from Galatians, sermonic movement born of juxtaposition is key.

Moreover, it should be noted here that preaching a sermon series (on this or any other set of texts) also requires the principle of juxtaposition (between itch and scratch, or then and now) to be manifest in a dual sense. That is, it needs to be observed (or shaped) in each sermon separately considered *and* maintained as connection among the several sermons. The preacher can become trapped in preaching a sermon series either by expecting that everyone heard last Sunday's sermon, or that the preacher does not need the ambiguity born of juxtaposition in each sermon. And sermon series are poorly conceived if in reality the preacher has in fact prepared one very long sermon which will take several weeks to complete. Classroom lecturers can get away with connections "to be continued" between different lectures, but not preachers with their sermons.

One of the critical issues for the preacher who chooses to do a sermon series is diversity. The matter is particularly acute with a book like Galatians because of the singular purpose of Paul's address. Much easier than this would be a sermon series from one of the synoptic gospels which could follow Jesus in his travels for several Sundays. In that case, the different people and episodes likely will raise quite different issues. Or again, even a longer Pauline epistle, such as one of his letters to the church at Corinth, will bring together a variety of concerns. But here, Christian liberty is the issue—or so it would seem. Hence, how does one find diversity in such singularity?

Our technique is to look for variations in his address. For example, what is the purpose of the Law represented here? Is it a matter of our needing a temporary custodian like children who are heirs—as the latter portion of chapter three suggests? Or is the Law a curse—as suggested in the earlier portion of the same chapter? Or, is the law a curse only when we rely on it? And if so, what might constitute "reliance"?

One of the important features involved in utilizing metaphor as Paul does here—beyond reaping its evocative power—has to do with the richness, the multivalence held within the parameters of metaphor. A good metaphor holds variances— sometimes apparent contradictions—within itself, which often open important homiletical doors.

Likewise, important homiletical issues can be raised by comparing the writing in question with other scripture texts—in this case even those written by the same author. For example, how does Paul characterize the law in his other writings? Does he always have this strongly negative reaction to the subject? If not, why not? Then again, there may be other biblical passages which will properly question Paul's view here. One of the most effective results of potential biblical conflict I have experienced occurred in Fred Craddock's sermon "Amazing Grace."[7] In his exploration of the connection between God's providence and human virtue, he cited numerous biblical texts, which say quite different things. Is it true that it is the good righteous people who never go hungry, or does it rain on the just and the unjust? Which will it be? Both ideas have biblical warrant. Craddock was wise not to argue with the validity of any text. He simply found another text to do the work.

The point here (beyond sermon technique, per se) is that when the preacher reaches deeply into a given text and explores its nuances with care, matters become nicely focused, particular and precise—which in turn leaves other passages full of other possibilities. Sermon series should avoid global themes, generally considered.

But in order to establish well a generative focus, it is important for us to observe another principle which emerges out of the difference between conflict and polar opposition. Conflict has to do with competing claims; polar opposition has to do with a favored and an unfavored option. People are seldom engaged by a discussion of good and evil, for they have already made that global decision—indeed, evidenced in their dutiful presence in the service of worship. Life is seldom marked by decisions simply between good and bad. Life is generally marked by choices involving competing goods. In a previous volume I noted how the classic western, "High Noon," has the marshall caught between his duty to defend his town and his word of honor proffered to his pacifist bride to relinquish his position in order for them to leave town for a new life together. Which good will he choose—his duty or his word of honor? Negatively put, shall we think of him as a liar or a coward?

Making certain that matters are shaped by competing claims rather than either/or opposites, with only one pole of acceptable choice, serves to deepen rather than expand the scope of any sermon. When we prepare to preach a sermon series this issue becomes even more critical.

Perhaps the most important consideration in contemplating the letter to the Galatians as a potential source of a sermon series is to remember that the more particular the writer's purpose the more likely that universals abound (even if underground). In the end, diversity is more powerfully accessible in the depth of the specific than in the range of the general.

The Coverup

*I Peter 2:19-25 (**Year A, Fourth Sunday of Easter**)*

It is difficult to understand why this text remains in the lectionary. It is one of those writings which at best *might once* have been suited to a very particular moment in the life of the early church. But, generalizing a truth out of context for use in the present century in the western world is virtually unthinkable.

The text in question involves an extraordinary exhortation to submissively endure suffering for Christ. In the second verse of the lection the text reads: "If you endure when you are beaten for doing wrong, what credit is that? But if you endure when you do right and suffer for it, you have God's approval" (2:20). What? Is this a text faithful to the gospel as we understand it? What kind of world order is being confirmed here? Should we presume corporal punishment is appropriate, indeed particularly commendable when we are being punished unfairly? Who in our time can identify with such treatment? The apparent irrelevance to current civilized understandings of justice is overwhelming.

No doubt the commentaries will remind us that this was written at a point of great persecution of the church *and* when expectations were high regarding the imminent coming of Christ. Given the unassailable structures of existing brutal power and the promise of deliverance soon to happen, this surely was good advice. Perhaps. But as an ongoing exhortation to the people of God centuries later—after the imminent return did not occur and has not occurred—and after centuries of experience of persecution suffered by the miserable of the earth, I think this can no longer be considered a proper admonition.

But is it not true that the Hebrew scriptures contain many similar texts of brutality—some viewed in fact as true to God's purpose? That is sometimes true, although you might note that great care has been given to exclude such material from the lectionary. For example, the carnage commanded by God of Elijah as reported in I Kings 19 (Year C, Proper 7) is thoroughly restructured by the revision committee which now "reversifies [the] texts to focus on the experience of the mountain."[8]

Often Old Testament passages involve a historical consideration of the people of God whose understanding of God continues to change, even in the canon. Simple exhortations like this one, however, do not provide such historical distancing. (The psalmist's word about the happiness coming to those "who take your little ones and dash them against the rock," Psalm 137:9, is appropriately excluded from the lectionary.)

What is even more peculiar about this passage is the explicit context which is named in the preceding verse. Perhaps you might have noticed that the lection begins with a connective: "For it is a credit to you if, being aware of God, you endure pain while suffering unjustly" (Psalm 137:19). The preceding verse makes things clear. As verse 18 instructs: "Slaves, accept the authority of your masters with all deference, not only those who are kind and gentle but also those who are harsh" (137:18).

Well, it is not difficult to understand why this verse is excluded. But now, to give directions for proper suffering in the context of slavery—all the while not revealing that context—is, I submit, a form of deceptive reduction. This kind of "out of context'' selection cannot be justified just because it results in a general humble point which finally is linked with the suffering of Christ. Preachers do this all the time, and the lectionary should not reinforce the habit.

Even more peculiar is the fact that, utilizing this same logic the lectionary committee has excluded I Peter 3:1-7, which begins: ''Wives, in the same way, accept the authority of your husbands'' (3:1). It is worth observing also that in the Revised Common Lectionary, Ephesians 5:21-33 regarding household codes which formerly appeared as Year B, Proper 16 has now been removed.

So what does the lectionary preacher do here? It should be ignored both as possible sermon text and also from the readings in the service. If something on suffering is desired, I suggest II Corinthians 1:1-7, which is a much more powerful statement. Rather than presume that God is pleased with or appeased by such suffering, the passage in II Corinthians announces hope: ''Blessed be the God and Father of our Lord Jesus Christ, the Father of mercies and the God of all consolation, who consoles us in all our affliction, so that we may be able to console those who are in any affliction with the consolation with which we ourselves are consoled by God. For just as the sufferings of Christ are abundant for us, so also our consolation is abundant through Christ'' (1:3-5). Incidentally, this Corinthian passage does not occur anywhere in the lectionary readings. I believe the replacement is in order. For those who might view this decision as inappropriate and, indeed, might wonder on what basis any preacher ought to presume to do such a thing, I will address such concerns in chapter three on norms for the lectionary preacher.

Noticing the Unnoticed

*Genesis 32:22-31 (**Year A, Proper 13**)*

This passage is incredibly rich in narrative power. It is the final segment of what is now a four-part lectionary sequence on Jacob. In the 1983 lectionary the three-part Jacob sequence jumped from the ladder episode to the Jabbok river experience. The new Revised Common Lectionary includes the marriage of Jacob to Leah and Rachel.

Each of the four passages are fast paced, powerfully imagistic, and eminently preachable. Indeed, they are a preacher's delight. I only wish the lectionary included more portions of the journey, such as the final treacherous blessing and the Mispah confrontation. In fact, later I will quarrel with the exclusion of the final blessing scene. But before we examine the entire sequence, let us attend to the concluding section—Jacob's wrestling match with the divine being. Surely, we can be satisfied with this lesson.

Overall, the answer is yes. The passage has narrative integrity. Its dramatic power is seldom equaled in the three-year lectionary. It is high drama. In its preached form, however, I believe it needs to have a slightly wider frame. Whether this opinion constitutes a critique of the pericope selection or simply a suggestion to preachers on how to develop the sermon is perhaps moot.

What I notice, however, is that the entire sweep of the Jacob story in general and this final episode in particular are not resolved into final denouement until the reunion of Jacob and Esau. Their conflict emerging in Rebekah's womb, his sojourn with uncle Laban—directly derivative of the ongoing conflict of Jacob and Esau—and now his return to the promised land cannot be complete without their embrace of reconciliation. But that occurs in the next chapter, verse 4. All of which means that the passage stops four verses too soon.

Yet, one might respond that this objection is valid if you are attending to the overall major plot line of his life. But this pericope focuses expressly on the sub-plot of the wrestling match. In one sense such a response is exactly on target. But, considered this way the sermon might miss a remarkable feature of the experience which empowers the listener enormously.

In terms of form we have here the wrestling match proper, together with a surrounding envelope, which could be imagined as *prelude* and *postlude*. Notice that immediately prior to our textual selection, and after receiving the scouting report of Esau coming with four hundred men, Jacob immediately divides the entourage of wives, servants, children, and flocks into two companies, "thinking, 'If Esau comes to the one company and destroys it, then the company that is left will escape' " (32:8). Clever. After a fearful prayer for deliverance, he passes out the gifts for Esau—call that *bribes*—together with instructions on what to say, and then Jacob takes his place—*behind everybody*. The picture is riveted in the mind. If worst comes to worst, Esau will have to kill half the total number before ever reaching Jacob. (Women and children first!) His instruction to them to give the gifts and say that "Jacob is behind us" (verse 20) is telling indeed.

. Moreover, when he camps at the Jabbok, note that he puts his wives, maids, and children on the Esau side of the river, while he is left alone on the safe side. Well, he thinks he is alone and safe—but he is wrong twice. *Now* we have the divine-human encounter, *after* we observe that Jacob is a wimp. But that is only one half of the envelope.

In the "postlude," what is the first thing he does as the journey commences on the morrow—and he sees Esau coming "and four hundred men with him" (33:1)? This time he divides wives, maids, and children, while "he himself went on ahead of them, bowing himself to the ground seven times, until he came near his brother" (33:3). He "went on *ahead*"? Indeed, he is the first to get to Esau, and no longer does anyone have to say: "Jacob is behind us." The shift from safety in the rear guard to vulnerability at the front line is a remarkable change of behavior. It is the wrestling match which lies between these different styles—together with a change of name. And the picture of change is vivid indeed, from walking normally but lagging behind, to walking with a limp and yet in front. True enough, the effect of the wrestling match is powerful. The envelope of prelude and postlude provides both vivid detail and credibility to the mysterious event.

Looking broadly at the sweep of the four passages, I have not so much a complaint as a preference. Given my stated views about the "requirement" of including the reunion of the brothers, it may seem ironic that I would now suggest replacing the first passage (Genesis 25:19-34, Year A, Proper 10) which recounts the twins' births and Esau's selling of his birthright to Jacob. Certainly this is the story's actual beginning—as clearly definable as is the reunion as the story's ending, except for one thing.

Narratively speaking, it is neither the births nor the birthright which is the driving force of the Jacob sequence. It is the trickery surrounding Isaac's final blessing which propels the story. This tale of treachery is a classic, easily among the handful of the canon's best. Its parabolic "more" is unsurpassed. And it is this episode which drives Jacob out of town fast, and, ironically, into Laban's lap. Moreover, the dream of the ladder is inexplicable without knowing why he is on the road. You will recall the deal he suggests to God—that if God will keep him fed and clothed and get him home *safely,* then he in turn will let God be God. And I think it clear that Jacbo's fear in his final return trip toward Esau is predicated exactly on that moment when Esau brought food for his father's dinner of final blessing only to discover that Isaac's stomach was already full of others' deceit and his heart empty of any further adequate word.

So central is this section, so irreplaceable, that it needs to be included. Easier it is, homiletically, to flash back quickly to mention their births than it is to flash forward to this pivotal scene. It should be the first reading of the sequence.

Finally, a word about the second pericope in the series—Genesis 28:10-19a. The Task Force for the newly Revised Common Lectionary has extended the versification to include verse 18 and part of 19, for the purpose of including Jacob's task of making a pillar the morning after his remarkable dream. But I regret that while extending the passage for narrative integrity, they did not finish the chapter (stopping only three verses short) to include the vow. The stone set in place, the oil on top, and the name *Bethel* are all nothing without the vow. It completes the episode *and* reveals Jacob's character. Without the whole piece here, the dream is limited to the innocence of campfire piety. But the terms he has in mind once awake are vintage Jacob: "If you will . . . then I will"—and even capped by a ten-percent tip. We need the vow here.

Watch What Is Missing

*Psalm 17:1-7, 15 (**Year A, Proper 13**)*

It may seem peculiar to find a discussion of a psalm. Is it not true that when we speak of the readings for a given Sunday, typically we have in mind three passages—the first lesson from the Old Testament, the second from the New Testament other than the Gospels, and the third and "controlling" lesson coming from the four Gospels? Indeed, in the May 1991 draft of the work of the Task Force on the Common Lectionary, the stated purpose of the inclusion of the psalms was quite specific: "The psalm of the day is understood primarily as a sung or congregational spoken act of praise rather than as a reading meant for homiletical purposes." Quickly, however the committee added (parenthetically), "though of course that need not be ignored."[9] Indeed, I think we are prone to categorize the psalms as properly belonging to liturgical pursuits and activities in a way which limits their full utilization and hence diminishes the life of the church. It is precisely the fact that the book of Psalms' "intrinsic spiritual depth and beauty have made it from earliest times a treasury of resources for public and private devotion''[10] that it is also a rich gold mine for the preaching task. Note how often, for example, that a funeral sermon is based on a psalm. Rather than delineate a prose/poetry dichotomy which limits our work, why not a both/and stance of inclusion? Besides, there are numerous other canonical hymns of the church which have been found homiletically powerful—the Magnificat, from the first chapter of Luke, for example, is probably the best known.

One need only recall the finely tuned narrative plot line of Psalm 139 or the pithy question-answer movement of Psalm 8 to sense the quickly accessible nature of the psalms for preaching. In particlar, the psalms waste no time naming the sermonic negative pole—the "itch." "How long, O Lord? Will you forget me forever?" asks Psalm 13. In case the issue is not heard quickly, the psalm provides fine rhythmic redundancy. So Psalm 13 continues: "How long will you hide your face . . . How long must I bear pain . . . How long shall my enemy be exalted . . . ? (verses 1b-2) One might name it "complication of the plot." By the end of that particular psalm, the world is turned upside down: "I will sing to the Lord because he has dealt bountifully with me" (verse 6). All in six verses! Indeed, the aesthetics of poetic form serve to compress the plot line. If there is anything a preacher might dream about for Sunday, it surely could be a text which has a compressed plot line.

It is precisely the poetic strength of the psalms, making them so useful in the liturgy, that additionally, makes them so powerful for preaching. Their potent expression of human emotion is ripe for sermonic work. Obviously this is not always the case, but comparatively judged with the rest of the canon, we make a fairly safe bet. But now to the psalm presently selected for our work here: Psalm 17:1-7, 15. In the ongoing work of the Task Force charged with revising the lectionary was the view that "twelve verses of a psalm seemed in general to be the appropriate number of verses to use.''[11] (One can imagine the impact upon narrative integrity if we observed that guideline for all the readings across three years' time.) Yet it must not have been a new idea, because the committee made no change in the Psalm 17 reading. The 1983 selection and the 1992 selection are the same—the reading simply was moved from Proper 8 to 13. (Incidentally, the several appearances of Psalm 139 include either verses 7-18 or verses 1-6 and 13-18, exactly twelve verses either way.)

Psalm 17 has fifteen verses, three too many, so a middle section was removed (long before the current revision). But why did they not count to twelve? Why does the reading contain only eight verses? Was there some other hermeneutical principle involved in the history of this particular pericope? Indeed there is a decided cast or tone to all the deleted verses, in fact a particular ingredient removed. And it just happens to be the central decisive contextual matter which governs the entire psalm. When removed, the psalm is wholly different reality.

The first seven verses of this psalm involve a plea for God to ''hear a just cause'' (17:1). The psalmist wants ''vindication'' (verse 2) and is quick to point out his virtues, for ''you will find no wickedness in me; my mouth does not transgress'' (17:3). Moreover, ''I have avoided the ways of the violent. My steps have held fast to your paths, my feet have not slipped'' (17:4b-5). So what does he desire? God's ''steadfast love'' (17:7) is the request. Quickly the lectionary reading jumps to the concluding verse: ''As for me, I shall behold your face in righteousness; when I awake, I shall be satisfied, beholding your likeness'' (17:15).

The psalmist certainly appears virtuous. His words of self-praise surely could be labeled arrogant. Who does he think he is, anyway? Can it really be that his steps ''have held fast'' to God's paths? Surely the psalmist's feet have slipped a bit. The spirit of this righteous claim here suggests that if not before, his feet are slipping *now* even as he speaks. Our reaction relates, however, not just to what the psalmist said but also to what others have deleted from what he said.

A look at the missing verses presents an entirely different picture and remolds the character of his claim. Verses eight through twelve make it clear. He is, in fact, under attack by "the wicked who despoil me, my deadly enemies who surround me" (17:9). Moreover, he is tracked down by adversaries who "like a lion [are] eager to tear, like a young lion lurking in ambush" (17:12).

Well, things do look different now, including his claim to innocence. It is, after all, one thing for a person to allege they are the best on the block, and quite another for a person in great adversity, even persecution, to ask "What is my fault?"

The cry of the psalmist's heart becomes credible in the awful presence of the enemy. He is not boasting; he is pleading. But when the enemy is removed from the reading, the psalmist's articulate cry sounds like so much boasting. So it is that by deleting verses eight through twelve, the psalmist is made a fool.

To be absolutely accurate, we should acknowledge that a small hint of trouble is included in the ending of verse 7 (but you can't stop in the middle of the sentence). That verse concludes with "O savior of those who seek refuge from their adversaries at your right hand." So the term *adversaries* is present in the reading which is given, but note the vague distance caused by the use of the third person. Without verses 8-12 one would not likely imagine it is the psalmist who is the real referent for the term *their*.

Beyond this, what specifically does the psalmist want in the cry for "steadfast love"? It becomes clear in verses 13 and 14. He wants deliverance, and he wants revenge. "By your sword deliver my life from the wicked" (verse 13). Indeed, in his present desperation the psalmist gets carried away by the very thought of divine intervention. "May their bellies be filled with what you have stored up for them'' (verse 14). The psalmist's imagination is still at work, wondering if God might just have some retribution left over for their children.

So the psalm's plot moves in the following fashion—from *just cause* to *request for help* in the context of *persecution* by means of *vindication* and *revenge* resulting in *satisfaction*. With verses eight through fourteen removed, the plot is radically different, moving from *bragging* to *request for help* for the sake of *satisfaction*. Quite a difference.

Should not the revenge be deleted on the same grounds we considered regarding the passage in I Peter? Perhaps, but there is quite a difference between the admonition there as to how we humans should behave and this request for God to behave as the psalmist decides.

It could be argued that for the lectionary reading to reveal the real occasion for this plea—the enemies—would require the request for specific divine action against them also to be included. Hence, the committee decision might be to avoid both enemies and divine action. But if so, the entire plot is gutted. Then why not include the verses about the horrible deeds of the enemies but simply jump over the retribution part into the final verse of resolution? Actually, one might envision such a remedy, with the result formed as follows:

12 They are like a lion eager to tear, like a young lion lurking in ambush.
15 As for me, I shall behold your face in righteousness; when I awake, I shall be satisfied, beholding your likeness.

Certainly this possible solution involves no more eisegesis than is presently provided, and we wind up with thirteen verses, closer to twelve than the eight which are now given. Or is there some other principle at work in the lectionary selection?

More important than verse count is the apparent decision to

avoid trouble altogether. This passage is viewed, after all, as liturgical assistance. Isn't it enough to have a pleasant psalm which asks simply to "give ear to my prayer" (verse 1b), "wondrously show your steadfast love" (verse 7a), and "I shall be satisfied" (verse 15b)? Pleasant praise is what we have been given—with apparent arrogance thrown in.

But I am reminded of the lectionary committee's commitment to principle number five regarding the use of the psalter: "Where the use of the full psalm is precluded for whatever reason, the selection taken ought to respect the integrity of the whole."[12] I think the revision committee should have changed this versification on their own grounds. But, for whatever reason, they chose to continue the reading as it had been given them by prior decision. The committee did not perpetrate anything here, they just did not correct it. So what should the preacher do?

Recently, I chose to read the lesson as given. With that as context, I began to complain about the psalmist's self-assessment—wondering whether anyone has a right to claim such virtue. I was hoping the congregation might identify with their own experience of people who think too highly of themselves. And it gave me an opportunity to use Pauline correctives to such thinking. This could become an opportunity for a bit of overhearing. The sermon's next move was to take note of the deleted portions (even providing a moment of comic relief at the expense of lectionary selectors by noting how trouble is often avoided).

The preached sermon made a decisive turn here as I began to "reconstruct" the character of the psalmist given our new data, and who now can be heard out of the desperate situation he is experiencing. Momentarily I mused about whether people's boasting might reflect a deeper and hidden pain.

Little wonder, then, the sermon suggested, that the psalmist hoped God would be as angry as he—and in fact do to those enemies what the psalmist would do if the chance were given.

The sermon moved finally to the psalmist's underlying confidence—not only of God's justice "if you try my heart, if you visit me by night" (verse 3), but knowing ultimately that "when I awake, I shall be satisfied, beholding your likeness" (verse 15).

The sermon's reprise noted that we do not know what eventually happened to these enemies, but ultimately, whatever are the "tears of the night" there shall be "joy in the morning" (from Psalm 30:5), because in the morning you may be certain of the presence of God. When preaching on Psalm 17, we follow the shape of movement from distress to hope—by means of opening conflict, complication, decisive turn, and denouement.

Even when one is unhappy with a given lection—sensing that a text has been botched—the preacher can utilize even the alleged cuts to help shape a sermon. Poor lectionary decisions can sometimes facilitate crucial and engaging insights for preaching. So it is that I suggest always to see what is happening around a text, note the context of its occurrence, and observe the lectionary shape in which it is given.

In wider perspective, we who preach need not avoid the psalter. Often we will be surprised by the riches we find. Indeed, as we explore the *four* readings that are given, the psalm may be our first choice for the sermon.

In this chapter we have explored numerous passages, noting in particular the difficulties faced by preachers attempting to generate sermons from lections. Hopefully, this has been an exercise in how to spot typical lectionary difficulties and how to overcome them homiletically. The goal, after all, is to reduce the liabilities often presented by the lectionary and, hence, better to reap the advantages of lectionary preaching.

This reconstruction prompts a further question. What are the ground rules that bear down upon anyone who presumes to preach? What hermeneutical principles or homiletical rules do we need to observe? What claims are presented to the preacher?

CHAPTER THREE

Claims Upon the Preacher

Having examined numerous lectionary passages which present differing problems for preaching, we now move to ask a more comprehensive set of questions. Apparently it is not enough for the preacher to worry about this Sunday's sermon—how to lure the given text into an effective homiletical shape which will prompt a hearing of the Gospel. Before Sunday dinner is complete, the preacher likely will be struck with the imposing reality that another Sunday is coming. And another, and another.

Beyond the question of what to do with the next set of "unlikely lections," the preacher may muse about the ongoing task itself. What are the principles or norms that continue to make claims upon the preacher, Sunday after Sunday? What set of homiletical assumptions, even if not consciously noticed, operate as regularly as the clock?

Of course, next Sunday's sermon will be different—a different text and a different pastoral agenda. Yet one trusts that there will be some common threads—of purpose, of homiletical strategy, of exegetical techniques, and of proclamatory hope. Every sermon is different; every sermon is the same.

The purpose of this chapter is to consider various claims which always get imposed upon the preacher, week after week. The list could be long. We will explore four: the claim of the text, the claim of the situation, the claim of sermon form, and the claim of the kerygma.

In order to facilitate the discussion, I propose we consider the fact that the canon has incredible theological diversity. One is likely to notice this fact next week when comparing those lections with the ones provided for last Sunday. And the preacher is caught, not only by the differing textual perspectives but also by shifting congregational needs. So, what does the faithful preacher do with this problem?

There are three tempting options available—each close at hand, each with some claim to legitimacy, *and each finally untenable*.

One can, of course, choose only the passages with which one agrees. Or, one can preach whatever theology happens to appear in the text for the coming Sunday. Or, again, one can simply take whatever pericope appears and twist it into the shape of the preacher's own point of view. Obviously, none of these three options will suffice, but they are "chosen" regularly just the same. It ought to be said, also, that each of these choices has some virtue to it—which, in part, accounts for its use.

I have no doubt that one of the reasons for not utilizing any lectionary at all—or at most, "dipping in" from time to time only—is for the purpose of safeguarding some kind of professional theological integrity. Certainly what is often alleged may be true, that each of us is tempted toward a few choice pithy passages we happen to like, much to be suffered by our congregations. Yet, this explanation is far too simple. Deeper than this stereotype is the plain truth that it is very difficult to preach what you do not believe, or to walk on egg shell phrases, such as "the writer obviously believed that . . . ," hoping that after the service no one will ask: "But, what do you believe?"

My own personal experience in the pew causes me to notice how often evangelical preachers favor the imperative exhortations of the Gospels while pastors in the Reformation tradition focus sharply on Paul. This may not be a fair generalization across the church, but this "leaning" has been true for me as listener. And should this not be the case? Although the idea of a canon within the canon is out of vogue at present, it is true for most of us that some passages are closer to the "bottom line," so to speak, or as Leander Keck articulated it, "the perceived center of the gospel and of the canon."[1] This "perceived center" in part reflects an ongoing tradition theologically, and even denominationally, in which the pastor participates. (As a liturgical heretic I have wondered from time to time while in the experience of worship why we did not *sit* for the reading of the Gospel and *stand* for the Epistle!) It is little wonder that many preachers are quite selective about the passages they choose to undergird their Sunday sermons.

The issue of theological integrity may also account for the fairly common experience of certain topical preaching that utilizes texts more for illustrative purposes than for sermonic grounding. Likewise, in hindsight I can see one reason why so many preachers in my youth were expository preachers, following the passage verse by verse with editorial comment. One's atomistic selectivity provided the *sense* of biblical preaching while actually preserving the last word for the preacher. Often, the preacher did not have to decide to be selective about what was said about each verse, it just happened to turn out that way. Again, at stake here is the integrity of the preacher's theological point of view. That is, until someone comes along with the rejoinder that our integrity is not the chief issue, the whole gospel is.

Which is the argument I hear regularly by those who choose the second "option"—namely, to preach whatever theology emerges from the passage. Canonical theological pluralism is a fact of life for all but the most literalist of preachers. One pastor told me recently about beginning a sermon by noting: "I don't particularly like this passage, in fact cannot really agree with it, but it is our Word for today."

At first blush, this approach seems an unlikely smorgasbord offering. If you're unhappy with today's dietary decision, wait until next week for a different menu—or is it a different chef? Surely, congregational confusion will be the result of such an approach.

Once again, however, a rather large issue is at stake. Is not the motif—"I must be true to my own theology"—a bit arrogant, after all? Clearly, the gospel is more comprehensive than our individual subjectivities. The call to be faithful surely must mean more than being faithful to oneself. One must be faithful to the Word whose canonical witness is multiple in points of view and forms of expression. Whoever linked Genesis 1:1–2:4a with 2:4b and following surely had more in mind than contradictions of order and forms of creations. Besides, says Keck, "the unity of the Bible is not uniformity in theology but constancy of perspective."[2] Well, one might question the evidence even of such "constancy."

The reduction of canonical pluralism into the integral position of the congregation's current pastor is, finally, to bear false witness to the life of the Church. The result this second "choice" attempts to avoid is the severe relativity of reinventing Christianity in every new age, or social group, or even single congregation.

Moreover, we may be dealing here with a kind of propositional literalism. The Good News of the gospel is never reducible to a short list of preachable canonical truths which are clean, clear, and conceptually covered by a single truth claim. "Respecting the diversity, particularity, and limitations of each writer," explains Keck, "frees one from the compulsion to make any given text say everything that is true, and allows the preacher to expound the gospel more fully across the span of time because no biblical writer put the whole truth into writing."[3] Every pastor who has preached at least six months knows that the "truth" this Sunday sounds sharply divergent from the "truth" preached a few weeks previously. Besides, what is true and needful for the congregation today may be quite different from the needs on another Sunday. At the same time, however, uncritical utilization of theologically diverse passages may, indeed, represent an abdication of pastoral responsibility. In fact, the issue here is not reducible simply to the question of the "whole truth," as though range of comprehensiveness accounts for the conflict. Often we are confronted by the divergence of conflicted texts, one of which claims a position clearly at odds with the viewpoint of another. Can a pastor legitimately switch theological hats each Sunday—this Sunday Matthean, next Sunday Pauline, and after that Johannine? Is this pastor a chameleon?

Sometimes those of us who believe we have managed to escape the homiletical traps of the first two options in effect have really unconsciously forged the third untenable option: namely to take whatever passage is presented and make it "say" what we want it to say. This option is quite easily accomplished—particularly if one does not think about it much. Eisegesis, after all, is seldom malicious. It just happens. The preacher, knowing in advance the heart of the gospel, sees it everywhere.

I recall well the moment I discovered that the prodigal son story really did not say what I had made it say. I had preached on the text many times, always focusing on that moment of grace when the father gives the robe of honor, the ring of authority, and the sandals of sonship—absolutely unmerited and unconditional. I preached it as Paul would have me preach. That is, until a colleague of mine reminded me that the father waited until the son repented and came back home. The father's gifts were in this sense conditional. No doubt Paul would have had the father leave the farm in the care of the elder son, head to the far country in search of his boy, and then rescue him from his bondage to the pig pen. Well, it certainly killed a fine sermon, until I read Helmut Thielicke's treatment of the parable. Obviously, he had faced the problem head on and concluded: "It wasn't that the son got so sick of the pig pen that he turned home; it was his understanding of home that made him so sick of the pig pen."[4] Whether that view "washes" or not will merit further thought. Certainly, one may rightfully claim that in the other two parables of Luke 15, the primary characters went searching for that which was lost—lamb and coin. But we tend to read into passages what we want. And there is a legitimate concern within the choice of this option too.

The fact that eisegesis happens with some regularity cannot be explained simply as a case of exegetically lazy pastors, nor does it revolve alone around our lack of self-conscious reflection. At stake here is the unity of God's revelation. Do we proclaim the Good News of the gospel—or do we offer the good news of multiple gospels—take your choice among Sunday offerings. If preaching is to occur in the context of the one, holy, catholic, and apostolic church then the term *one* ought to mean something about God's self-revelation. Are we not called to rightly divide the word of truth? Surely preaching is meant to be truth through personality. Nonetheless, all of us know that disheartening experience of discovering in the course of our exegetical work, that a passage simply will not enable the homiletical turn for which we yearned, and thought we found.

Hence, if one cannot simply "ride" a few selected texts for the sake of theological integrity, if one cannot present cafeteria selections in order to be faithful to canonical pluralism, and if one is not free to twist (interpret) whatever passages are used to the preacher's own viewpoint, even if unitary doctrines of revelation and ecclesiology are desirable, is there another option?

Is there some kind of blend to all three unsatisfactory choices? Can one be true to revelation, text, and self all at once? Every Sunday? What set of interpretive principles can we fashion here that might be helpful? Can this matter be resolved successfully?

I believe the answer is both a *yes* and a *no*. By *yes* I refer to the obvious mandate imposed by the awesome task of preaching. We simply must adhere to interpretive norms for preaching—a kind of homiletical hermeneutic.

By *no* I refer to the vulnerable ever-changing moments of the preaching event. If there were absolutely certain rules with clear guarantee attached we would not need this discussion. No set of norms can remove our vulnerability. No *interpretation* is divinely revealed. As professor of New Testament, Lindsey Pherigo said repeatedly to students: "The preacher has the choice of proclaiming that which is partially untrue or of being quiet altogether." R. E. C. Browne identifies "the essential untidiness of the gospel."[5] It is simply not the case as alleged by a recent preacher at an annual conference session of The United Methodist Church, that in effect: "Although seminary professors present may choose to quibble over interpretation, if God says it, that's good enough for me."

Given the liabilities of the three claims above, I hazard the following interpretative principles, norms, or claims for preaching.

The Claim of the Text

We focus first on textual norms because, to begin with, this book is about lectionary preaching in which the pericopes are established in advance. Also, beginning with the text is for me the normative procedure. Granted, situational concerns of the congregation and world may helpfully prompt the initial phases of any given sermon preparation. H. Grady Davis even spoke favorably about the sermonic idea which although not "found in the Bible in so many words, . . . may still be biblical, and may honestly be preached with biblical sanction."[6] I have no problem with such approaches unless they become the usual practice. Normatively, the text is the place of beginning.

Surely it has been clear for us all, long before our present consideration, that no one is free to manipulate a text at will. Such sermonic bootlegging is wrong no matter how worthy the cause. Often one sees this "noble" yet untenable practice happen in the expository handling of Old Testament material, which gets pressed into christological service. Claims for trinitarian understanding in Old Testament usage of the divine editorial "we," for example, deserve our greatest suspicion. More likely, however, than this blatant kind of eisegesis is the careless homiletical use of Old Testament lections provided for the Advent and Lent seasons. The sheer fact of their choice by others may lure us into false connections of meaning. Sometimes those "others" may be a lectionary committee.

Certainly Old Testament scholar Charles Baughman is correct when he asserts that all Christians read the Hebrew scriptures through the lens of the Incarnation. This *ought* to be the case. But as he observes the companion piece to this fact of faithful life, however, ought to be *noticing* and acknowledging this fact. Such self-conscious reflection should result in the preacher's capacity for differentiating the separable commitments of biblical writer and preacher. Likewise, this differentiation needs sometimes to be included explicitly in the sermon itself. Faithfulness to the text, however, is not as simple a matter as it may appear, nor is it the last word.

Faithfulness to the text should not mean, for example, an all too quick turn to the experts for their judgment. I have suggested in a previous book (*How to Preach a Parable*) that an active and direct search for the meaning of the text is not properly the first step in sermon preparation. There I suggest a preliminary process of reading the text aloud in numerous translations, as well as utilizing a number of other techniques calculated to keep us out of the driver's seat.

This advice may first appear at odds with my claim here regarding textual faithfulness. Should we not begin the process of sermon preparation by hard exegetical work? I have learned not to do this. The task of exegesis is best engaged *after* certain preliminary steps have been completed. The key is to allow the text to wash over and through us before we start washing it with our own agenda. To be sure, there are some preachers who appear quite unable to release their grip on orthodoxy long enough to be freely washed with just any apparently unorthodox text. As a result, even the preliminary washing may be badly infected with preconceived truth. My experience is, however, that if we begin engaging the text at the point of issues and problems rather than answers, themes, and meaning, we are far less likely to impose our own agenda of convictions.

Nor is faithfulness to the text synonymous with faithfulness to the author's intent. The author's intent is what launched the text. Once launched into history it often has a mind of its own. The original author is a midwife, not a final arbiter. Indeed, the text will sometimes turn on its author with appropriate judgment. Every preacher has experienced that powerful moment when a parishioner will turn a sermon back on the preacher for application, saying: "But pastor, didn't you also say in the same sermon that. . . ?"

Contemporary use of Paul's motif from Romans (10:3) that "there is no distinction" is a case in point. And by the very wording of the passage from Galatians one can properly infer that Paul did not mean to disestablish slavery as a social reality when he said "there is no longer slave or free" (Galatians 3:28). He only said the differing realities make no ultimate difference with God. Yet that passage can be applied properly against slavery and other contemporary forms of racial injustice. The power of such passages is not limited to the author's intent. Nor should faithfulness to the text result in a kind of propositional idolatry.

I am constantly amazed to hear preachers who would never reduce revelation to propositional truth but nonetheless adhere to the letter of the law in handling a text. Though rejecting theological fundamentalism, they succumb to lectionary fundamentalism. In effect they apparently operate on the principle that if the pericope says X, the sermon must proclaim X. I have been helped greatly by González and González's suggestion that often we must look to the direction or "leaning" of the text more than to its literal statement.[7] In short, faithfulness to the text must take into account the cultural context in which it is found. And there is no way to find the "kernel of truth" without the encumbrance of cultural, linguistic, and cosmological views. They are the shape the truth is taking. Translation to our time has to do with reshaping, not disembodying. David Buttrick says it well: "What is the text trying to do" rather than what is it trying to say.[8] Then, one must take the next step in asking: What does the text now want to do?

One adjustment or clarification is needed here. While the text has a life of its own, sometimes moving beyond the intention of the writer, it should not be viewed in isolation. There are those scholars of narrative criticism, such as Mark Ellingsen, who when considering preaching have no interest in such a historical-critical issue as "determining the text's 'situation-in-life.' "[9] Or, as Mark Allan Powell explains: "The real author and the real reader are diagrammed as lying outside the parameters of the text itself."[10] We are left with an implied author and an implied reader, both revealed from inside the text.

While one can appreciate the commitment to focus "on the nature of the text as literature"[11] rather than simply as a means or window to something else "more important," one needs to be cautious regarding the apparent negation. As David Bartlett notes so clearly regarding the writing of Paul: "It does make a difference in interpreting the texts whether the people to whom they were addressed were primarily outcasts or modestly upwardly mobile, or some of each. The texts by themselves do not tell us that."[12] Surely, we are enriched both by historical-critical *and* narrative scholarship.

Nonetheless, the beginning point for the lectionary preacher is the text that is given. It makes a legitimate claim upon all who would preach. It is not, however, the end of the matter. It is the first of at least four claims to be pressed upon the preacher who is moving toward the Sunday sermon.

The Claim of the Situation

The proper claim of the text for our faithfulness is just the beginning. Faithfulness to the situation of the preaching event is an equally legitimate claim.

The Word never exists in a vacuum. Truth does not *exist,* it *relates to.* Revelation is a historical event, not a "timeless truth" as such. As H. Richard Niebuhr reminded us, revelation occurs within community. So the second chapter of his classic book *The Meaning of Revelation* is entitled "The Story of Our Life."[13] His reference here is specifically biblical, but its validity did not cease with the closing of the canon. We all live in particular communions. Lutherans appear to discern God's revelation regarding law and gospel with a different kind of clarity than those of us in the Wesleyan tradition. Moreover, all of us are gifted by a tradition of biblical scholarship which helps shape the receipt of revelation. In "Narrative Theology" Gabriel Fackre notes that story exists on three levels—canonical, community, and personal.[14] Typically, the revelatory moment occurs when these three levels become as one. Revelation is a historical and communal event.

Although some preachers may worry about relativizing the biblical message by paying too much attention to the biblical context, few have difficulty shaping a sermon to fit the perceived needs of the congregation. This is particularly well-understood by those who serve more than one congregation at the same time. Pastors of multiple congregations bear witness, either to how they change the sermon in the car while traveling from the 9:30 to the 11:00 A.M. service, or confess that it simply happens automatically as they look out over the congregation during the second sermon. Of course the same principle was at work at the birth of the text.

Paul is a good model here. What, exactly, is his understanding of the law as contrasted with the gospel of grace? In part it depends on the congregation to whom he is writing. Sometimes his view seems even to shift during the writing. Is the law a covenant of condemnation or a temporary guardian? The answer is, "yes it is." When does participation in the Jewish legal system enable one to be all things to all people and when is it a matter of ultimate insincerity which must be confronted face to face? This is not a question that is answerable by reference to "eternal truth." The truth cannot be imagined outside the context of time and place.

Keck explains that "to preach biblically is to take full account of the concrete issues to which the text was addressed in the first place; it is to reckon with the fact that what the biblical writers found necessary to say was determined not by truth in general but by needs in particular."[15] In terms of lectionary preaching the historical situation of the hearers—denominationally, culturally, psychologically, and politically—participates in the question of what a text "means." Which is the reason that North American Christians may be (should be) amazed by textual meaning when mediated by the peasants of Nicaragua in *The Gospel in Solentiname*.[16]

Likewise, every pastor knows the experience of planning a sermon, for example, that is appropriately focused on the "criticizing" pole, as Walter Brueggemann would describe it,[17] and based faithfully on the text, which becomes inappropriate, even false, because of some event that happens within the congregation's life late in the week. The "point" when considered outside the context of the listeners may indeed be unassailably true. But, now it becomes untrue, not the Word, for Sunday.

If God's revelation is historical and relational more than propositional, then the context of time and place helps shape the meaning of any utilized text. Surely the writer of Luke must have understood the norm of faithfulness to the situation when he took the passage about wine and wineskins from Mark and added an extra line. "No one after drinking old wine desires new wine" (Luke 5:39), says the writer, because in fact "the old is better" (KJV). The additional line certainly alters the point being made, by approximately 180 degrees. Now, which version is "true," Mark's or Luke's? The moment one answers by reference to the "purpose of the writing," one has underscored the interdependency of textual truth and situational claim.

Indeed, there are texts in the lectionary which at a given time and place, simply ought not be used. It is possible that none of the lections can be used and remain faithful both to the text and to the situation. I recognize that this opens the door to the ever-present danger that the preacher will become an accommodator with seldom a passage quite right for "where the congregation is at this point in time." For some, this chronic ailment is a spinal problem more than a preaching dilemma. It simply *surfaces* in the sermon, and everywhere else.

At this point in time and in this context, I am more concerned with those would-be faithful lectionary preachers who are going to be true to the text if it kills them—and us.

Moreover, there is a difference between the preaching office and the teaching office. Although both are engrafted to the kerygma—as Grady Davis was quick to point out—their functional forms are different. There is a time and place to carefully explore a text—its problems and possible contradictions, its difference from other texts on the same subject—and the pulpit may not be the proper place. A bible study may be just right. As mentioned earlier, one of the tremendous assets of the lectionary is the many ways it evokes the study life of the congregation.

Some passages from the lectionary simply cannot be preached on some occasions without distorting the continuing revelation of God. When that carefully considered occasion occurs, the passage should be replaced by another, inside or outside of lectionary pericopes.

Every preacher has a solemn obligation to be faithful to the text *and* to be faithful to the body of Christ locally expressed, the community of faith that has entrusted the preaching task to one who they believe can discern the Spirit. But faithfulness to the text and faithfulness to the setting does not complete our obligations. The preacher must also be faithful to the claims of that particular art form called the sermon.

The Claim of Sermon Form

At first blush, it may seem strange to include sermon form as one of the four primary claims which the lectionary preacher must engage. The authority of the text and the legitimacy of the lived experience of the congregation stand outside the creative work of the pastor in sermon preparation and delivery. Likewise, the nature of the gospel (the fourth claim, yet to be discussed) has a transcendent quality about it. These claims each make a demand on the preacher's work. One is held accountable to them. Sermon form, as the final shape of the preaching event, seems an entirely different matter. Is it not simply the container that these other concerns fill? Is it not simply the willing servant of text, congregation, and kerygma, around which these other realities happen to converge? Well, if so, the "container" has a shape, and the "servant" has rights. Sermon form is not a vacuous nonentity known only by the company it keeps, nor a neutral warehouse of infinite possibilities just waiting to be raided.

Indeed, for some the term *sermon* is an omnibus category, nicely defined by whatever "works." So, one hears it said: "I would rather see a sermon than hear one any day." Which is a lot like the adage: "A picture is worth a thousand words"—to which I respond: "only after you have the thousand words in place." Likewise, no one quite knows how to "see" a sermon until having had some experience in hearing them. All of this, mind you, is far from academic. Could an effective pantomime become a sermon? How about an impressive dance? One can answer *yes* only with the help of a metaphoric tease.

The moment one seriously considers any other art form, the issue becomes apparent. Canvas art involves conventions or rules regarding form, line, and color. Music is limited to certain forms of sound. While both are beholden to other claims, such as the artist's purpose and the occasion for the piece of work, they also impose their own parameters upon the world. So does the sermon. The fact that these "internal" claims are subject to historical alteration only serves to underscore their power.

Certainly, there are innumerable other ways to proclaim the gospel. The sermon is only one, but it *is* one—and it has a life of its own, with rules and conventions. Whenever other claims are entertained, they do not simply "take over" the shaping of the sermon like some bully. They incorporate themselves inside the form a sermon takes.

For example, it is often said that the literary genre of the text determines the shape of the resultant sermon. Nonsense. If this were true then preaching a sermon on the Lord's Prayer would of necessity have to begin with "Let us pray." Likewise, preaching from an epistle would result in the pastor announcing that since the text is a letter, "the ushers will now distribute my written piece of correspondence to you."

Some of us who are advocates of narrative preaching are sometimes told that narrative sermons are appropriate *only if* the biblical passage being utilized happens to be in narrative form. Some even contend that story may not be appropriate because "some people have no story."[18] But, what about the One who is alpha and omega, the beginning and the end? (Perhaps someone should have told the writer of I Peter that because "once you were no people" obviously you cannot be the people of God.)

The point here is *not* that the preacher ignores the literary genre of a biblical text. To do so would be both foolish and irresponsible. The point *is* that the biblical literary forms are not the final arbiter of homiletical shape. The homily is a different art form. To insist otherwise is like complaining that a canvas artist failed to include any words in an acrylic rendering of a person in prayer. It surely ought not be an occasion for rebuke that a composer insists upon staying within the limited medium of notes, because notes are the central shape music takes.

Although, like other forms of art, the sermon's rules and conventions become altered through time, there are, nonetheless, some commonalities amidst the changes. For example, in the last century in North America, some dramatic changes have taken place in sermonic shape. Lucy Rose, for one, has identified a dominant shift, recognizable sequentially in the work of John Broadus, H. Grady Davis, and Fred Craddock.[19] Richard Eslinger speaks of a "paradigm shift" from rhetoric to narrative.[20] I would identify this major change as one somewhat analogous to a shift of figure and ground. That is, a century ago preachers followed Aristotle's rhetorical priniciples, spiced within by touches of poetics. Now the encompassing envelope is, for some, narrative in shape with rhetorical devices occurring inside the narrative envelope.

In the present discussion, the larger issue is to note that there are indeed principles at work here, and variables at play in the sermonic endeavor. These principles make a claim born of their own integrity. To be more specific:

A sermon is a temporal bridging event by means of oral discourse aimed toward the experience of revelation.

A sermon involves actual human speech. Like music, it happens in time. (A sermon manuscript found in the narthex is only what is left over after the sermon has already happened.) The fundamental sermonic aim is the hope of a revelatory moment of some kind. Other goals are included, of course. Sometimes catechetical instruction is included. Brueggemann may intend to energize a vision of alternative consciousness. Fosdick would hope for group counseling to occur. Buttrick would desire the listeners' consciousness to be shaped. Barth would insist on a faithful witness, whatever God might choose to do with it. Whether the preacher is supposed to create it, evoke it, or bear witness to it, will depend in part on one's theology of preaching. But in any case, the aim, the hope is connected with what we believe to be God's self disclosure. If the sermon is not calculated to do that, it is not a sermon. It may be a lecture on a religious subject; it may be a celebrative invoking of group memory. But participation in the Word is key. Rules, strategies, and conventions can be defended only in light of this key.

To claim that a sermon is a *bridging event* is to prompt our naming of a set of rules and conventions potentially operative in the homiletical art form. Actually, we have been utilizing such norms already throughout this writing. Here, we need only to be reminded.

Earlier we observed that the shape a sermon takes always involves closing a gap (see p. 17). Sermons *do something* by definition—whether solving, mediating, or elucidating. There is always a move *from* one reality *toward* another. *Itch; scratch. Before; after.* How conventions of the art shift while still observing this norm can be readily discerned by noting the difference between deductive and inductive preaching.

The deductive sermon moves from generalization to specific explication. The inductive sermon moves from specific factors to generalization. The one is the reverse of the other, but *both move*. (In this limited sense at least, it could be said that both are narrative in shape.) The preacher must discern which movement maximizes participation and facilitates the intended result. The title of Fred Craddock's first book, *As One Without Authority,* suggests how one crucial variable impacts the overall claim of homiletical form.

But you say, the given biblical text does not make any move; it is simply a grocery list of virtues. Cannot one simply recount, perhaps amplify the set of virtues and call it a sermon? No, but one might call it a lecture.

Again, our remembering the several scriptural passages considered in chapter two helps us discern how the claim of sermonic form sometimes requires correction of the given lection. Indeed, several norms of sermonic form are at stake in these passages.

With the pericope in Jonah, the exclusion of the full range of action precluded the appropriate *bridging event.* That exclusion also puts at risk the homiletical norm of sermonic *depth.* The Galatians selections tend to remove the impact of the "before" sections. Another norm of sermon form is *unity,* which is hard to fulfill when bereft of the missing sections. I Peter ignored the theological integrity of the preacher. How can the homiletical demand for *relevant correspondence* with the congregation be accomplished through the use of this text? The passages in Jacob did not move to actual denouement. The norm of *internal cohesion* is jeopardized. The response in the Psalm distorted motive. Hence, a sermon shaped by the limitations of that given pericope would fail the test of *unity.* In all these cases, the requirements of effective sermon form make their claim.

Clearly sermonic form is not some kind of blank slate which only passively awaits other claims. Yet one must not elevate the claim here. It does not exist in a vacuum. It is not the last word. But its word does have a rightful place.

Like any other kind of artist, the preacher must first become a disciplined servant of the art form, whose rules and conventions serve not only as limiting parameters, but also as facilitators for creative freedom.

Of course the text makes its claim. The situation makes its demand. So does the art form itself—with norms, conventions, and strategy born out of its own integrity. But there is yet another claim, both transcending and yet unifying the other claims. It is the claim of the gospel.

The Claim of the Gospel

This transcendent claim is the bottom line of preaching. With text in hand within the context of the gathered congregation, and by means of sermonic shape, the preacher is called to proclam the Word. What is most clear is that no one, two, or all three of the other claims have the last word for the preaching event. Nor do all three claims harmoniously fused together constitute the preached word. This additional consideration has controlling claim.

Put bluntly, we are not called to preach biblical texts. We are called to proclaim the Word. Our first obligation is not to address the needs of the congregation. It is to announce the good news of the gospel. Obviously the text should facilitate our witness. Clearly the needs of the congregation form the context of our work. But there is not a simple one-to-one correlation of proclamation to either text or congregation.

Preaching, normatively speaking, bespeaks participation in the Word of God. The term *Word,* of course, may refer to preaching, or to the written canon, or to Christ, depending upon the context. Although both the canon and the proclaimed word from the pulpit are subordinate to the Word made flesh, each is a participative witness to the primacy of God's act in Christ. And this is indeed heady company for the Sunday sermon to keep. Just as the church is called to be the continuing incarnation, so the sermon is called to participate in God's continuing revelation. Hendrikus Berkhof goes so far as to claim that "the sermon mediates salvation,"[21] being "the third institutional medium of the Church."[22]

Theologically, my preference is to approach the issue less formidably with Canon R. E. C. Browne, who says that "ultimately the preacher's work is to help people to be in a state of mind where perception is possible, that is, in a state where their minds are open and receptive to the divine action."[23] Indeed, the sense of "divine action" is critical here in understanding what we are about. At the same time, we ought not forget his other conviction at this point, that "in a sense the sermon does not matter, what matters is what the preacher cannot say because the ineffable remains the ineffable and all that can be done is to make gestures toward it with the finest words that can be used."[24]

The mandate for preaching is to announce once again, as best we can, the Reign of God, in the hope that God will make of it a revelatory moment, which as Niebuhr puts it, is "that special occasion which provides us with an image by means of which all the occasions of personal and common life become intelligible."[25]

But, how is all of this somehow beyond the questions of text and situation? Is it not the case that preachers unite the text's message and the people's need? No, it is not. The text's meaning alone may not be the Word's claim for Sunday—and answering people's needs may fall considerably short of announcing the Reign of God.

It is difficult to name precisely my meaning here, but every preacher understands it Sunday after Sunday. One's biblical work is a necessary but not sufficient ingredient in sermon preparation. Every preacher does more than look, explore, study, and then transcribe the results. There is an expectant waiting involved in sermon preparation. As Frederick Buechner describes it, the preacher "listens out of the same emptiness as [the listeners] do for a truth to fill [them] and make [them] true."[26]

Every preacher knows what it means to wait—expectantly.

We wait, not simply to understand thoroughly what the text is saying, or even doing. We wait wondering what God may have in store for our people come Sunday. Hence, it is not enough to note that the biblical message "is many faceted,"[27] as William Carl correctly advises, or to observe that all New Testament theologies "point to Christ,"[28] or explain that "the unity of the Bible is not uniformity in theology, but constancy of perspective."[29] The truth is closer to Gardner Taylor's observation that "when we have touched some of the depths that are in us we are at the threshold of the room where true preaching occurs and which engages people at the profound levels of their existence."[30]

Hopefully, that other room is prompted by the text. It is not likely identical with it. We wait for the Word. Keck notes that the content of whatever passages are in question "must itself be assessed theologically and morally, and in light of the perceived center of the gospel and of the canon."[31] No wonder we wait. Moreover "because that meaning is found by discernment and insight rather than by applying principles or following rules of interpretation. . . . Only in retrospect does it become clear what was going on in the interpretative process."[32] No wonder Berkhof says that the "unity of Scripture does not lie in itself but in the oneness of the God who remains the same in the continually changing encounter."[33]

Specifically, the text is the *primary prompter* but not the final arbiter. Most of the time the text's meaning, when thoroughly and properly explored, is sufficient to evoke a word out of the silent waiting. But sometimes it is more a *preliminary prompter,* rather than a primary one. That is, the issues generated by the text may need further biblical grounding, even by another supplemental text, in order for the Word to become evoked. On rare occasions, the text may need to be supplanted altogether. This is what is meant by my previous assertion that we are not called to preach the text, but rather to preach the gospel.

Now, of course, a significant temptation lurks here. It is possible for a preacher regularly to find a text "wanting" and then quickly move to another more "compatible" with the preacher's own leanings. On the other hand, not to run that risk may be to open the door to another one; namely, a kind of textual idolatry. As Browne concludes: "If the biblical writers are held to be free agents who used their imagination and intelligence in obedience to the divine promptings to say the greatest things about God and [human beings], then . . . preacher[s] must look on [their] work accordingly."[34]

Likewise, the claim of the situation does not involve a simple one-to-one relation with the preached word either. Barth articulates the matter sharply: "If the congregation brings to church the great question of human life and seeks an answer for it, the Bible contrari-wise brings an answer, and seeks the question corresponding to this answer."[35] Barth's reasoning is that often the stage of human life out of which the question emerges "is not yet acute."[36] Hence, the Bible transforms the question, giving it "its first real depth and meaning—and in a way that leads even the most frightened, the most humbled, and the most despairing . . . [person] to the edge of a worse abyss than . . . [ever] dreamed of."[37]

Of course, not every preacher shares Barth's assessment of the human predicament! Yet, it is nonetheless true, that inevitably there is a pastoral adaptation or reinterpretation to human needs as articulated and presented by the congregation. Whatever the relative position, the preacher's waiting for the Word is prompted not only by a presenting text but a theological understanding of the presenting needs. If it is true, as Brueggemann insists that "the royal consciousness leads people to numbness, especially to numbness about death,"[38] then obviously reliance on the congregation's perception of need is inadequate for the preaching event. Consequently, "it is the task of prophetic ministry and imagination to bring people to engage their experience of suffering.''[39] Indeed, one of the central purposes of preaching has to do with *naming* human experience. The pulpit tends to be long on advice and short on diagnosis. Human experience is not always self-evident and people often only half experience their own personal events because they do not have a way, theologically and linguistically, to identify them. Often one of the first steps to relevant preaching is to fully reveal what is going on. Indeed, the preacher may be at a loss for constitutive language, too, until a text is brought into juxtaposition with people's lived experiences.

As long as the text is examined only at surface level—''what does it say?''—and the congregational situation is accepted at face value—''What do we think we need?''—the lectionary sermon will likely remain at the level of good advice. To both text and situation comes the claim of the kerygma—never quite what was expected, and re-birthed in the depths of waiting.

Likewise, the claim of sermon form must yield to the claim of the gospel. The perceived shape of the sermon will determine just how this interaction occurs. For example, for those who think that narrative preaching is really story preaching, the overarching claim of the gospel will come quickly—with someone suggesting that some issues require ''hard critical thought,'' not ''just a story.'' But if one believes as I do that narrative preaching essentially involves a *basic principle* of plot-like process, then when to abandon or alter this sermonic shape is more complicated. Yet, there are times when the kerygmatic claim demands it.

For example, those familiar with my work on the shape of narrative plot, will know that the basic structure of narrative preaching involves a complication of an opening conflict. But what about a funeral sermon? Well, things are complicated enough already. Indeed, complicating the plot at such a moment actually inflicts unnecessary pain, and furthermore, requires a kind of involved investment of the listeners that is not productive, or sometimes even possible. In such a case the preacher would do well to focus on Hope with simplicity and biblical grounding—period. The Good News requires it.

It is important to our exploration of the claim of the gospel to note what is *not* meant, not intended here. One does not ride roughshod over lectionary texts, coercing them to appear to say what the preacher wants to get across. Nor should the preacher make a point of ignoring the human situation within the congregation for the sake of alleged kerygmatic purity. The relationships of the various claims are more subtle, more profound.

It is not as though the gospel claim is a new, utterly separate ingredient, added to three others. It is more like the transcendent dimension *of* the others—when text, situation, and proclamatory form come together in revelatory harmony. One does not invent a vision of the Reign of God; one reclaims the vision—as Brueggemann would say.[40] The church does not construct a new harmony; it receives the promise that is given again, which evokes the "communion which makes us human."[41] We who preach do not craft the words; we stumble onto them—ever longing for a hint of congruity with the ineffable—waiting for the surprise of a door to be opened, just a crack, so that light may flood the darkness.

Notes

CHAPTER ONE: *Liabilities and Assets of Lectionary Preaching*

1. "The Use of the Bible in the Lectionary." *Societas Liturgica* (April 1992), pp. 6-9.
2. Horace T. Allen, from an unpublished paper presented to the *Societas Liturgica* 1991 in Toronto, Ontario.
3. See Harry Emerson Fosdick, *The Living of These Days* (New York: Harper & Brothers, 1956).
4. See Karl Barth, *The Word of God and the Word of Man* (New York: Harper & Row, 1957), pp. 97-135.
5. David G. Buttrick, "Interpretation and Preaching," *Interpretation* (January 1981), p. 54.
6. Paul Scott Wilson, *Imagination of the Heart* (Nashville: Abingdon Press, 1988), p. 127.
7. Merill Abbey, "Crisis Preaching for the 70s," *Pulpit Digest* (February 1971), pp. 7-12.
8. Robert Bolton, "No Lectionary for Me," *Pulpit Digest,* (November 1991), pp. 7-9.
9. Justo L. González and Catherine Gunsalus González, *Liberation Preaching* (Nashville: Abingdon Press, 1980), p. 40.
10. *Ibid.*
11. *Ibid.*
12. Fred B. Craddock, *Preaching* (Nashville: Abingdon Press, 1985), p. 106.
13. Andrew W. Blackwood, *Planning a Year's Pulpit Work* (New York: Abingdon Press, 1942).
14. Fred B. Craddock, *Overhearing the Gospel* (Nashville, Abingdon Press, 1978), p. 112.
15. *Ibid.*
16. *Ibid.*

17. Wilson, p. 34.
18. Paul Tillich, *Dynamics of Faith* (New York: Harper & Brothers, 1956).
19. Jess Stein, ed., *The Random House Dictionary* (New York: Random House, 1967), p. 1221.
20. *Ibid.,* p. 1360.

CHAPTER TWO: *Overcoming the Obstacles of Lectionary Preaching*

1. Paul Scott Wilson, *Imagination of the Heart* (Nashville: Abingdon Press, 1988), p. 34.
2. Eugene L. Lowry, *How to Preach a Parable* (Nashville: Abingdon Press, 1989).
3. Fred B. Craddock, *As One Without Authority* (Enid, Oklahoma: Phillips University Press, 1974; Abingdon Press, 1979), pp. 51-76.
4. *The New Oxford Bible* (New York: Oxford University Press, 1973), p. 1410.
5. David L. Bartlett, "Story and History: Narratives and Claims," *Interpretation* (July 1991), p. 239.
6. Ibid., p. 232.
7. Fred B. Craddock, "Amazing Grace," *Thesis* (Pittsburgh: Thesis Theological Cassettes, June 1976.
8. Andy Langford, unpublished notes of the Task Force on the Common Lectionary, "The Revised Common Lectionary: 1992." (May, 1991), p. 111.
9. *Ibid.,* p. 21.
10. *Oxford Bible,* see note 4, p. 6560.
11. Langford, see note 8, p. 24.
12. Langford, *Ibid.*

CHAPTER THREE: *Claims Upon the Preacher*

1. Leander E. Keck, *The Bible in the Pulpit* (Nashville: Abingdon Press, 1978), p. 122.
2. *Ibid.,* p. 107.
3. *Ibid.,* p. 109.
4. Helmut Thielicke, *The Waiting Father* (New York: Harper & Brothers, 1959), pp. 26-27.
5. Robert E. C. Browne, *The Ministry of the Word* (Philadelphia: Fortress Press, 1976), pp. 58-71.
6. Henry Grady Davis, *Design for Preaching* (Philadelphia: Fortress Press, 1958), p. 48.
7. Justo L. González and Catherine Gunsalus González, *Liberation Preaching* (Nashville: Abingdon Press, 1980), pp. 82-89.

8. David Buttrick, *Homiletic: Moves and Structures* (Philadelphia: Fortress Press, 1987), pp. 285-303.
9. Mark Ellingsen, *The Integrity of Biblical Narrative* (Minneapolis: Fortress Press, 1990), p. 62.
10. Mark Allan Powell, *What Is Narrative Criticism?* (Minneapolis: Fortress Press, 1990), p. 19.
11. *Ibid.*, p. 8.
12. Bartlett, p. 235.
13. H. Richard Niebuhr, *The Meaning of Revelation* (New York: The Macmillan Company, 1941), pp. 32-66.
14. Gabriel Fackre, "Narrative Theology: an Overview," *Interpretation* (October 1983), pp. 340-352.
15. Keck, p. 115.
16. Ernesto Cardenal, *The Gospel in Solentiname, Vol. 1* (Mary Knoll, New York: Orbis Books, 1976).
17. Walter Brueggemann, *The Prophetic Imagination* (Philadelphia: Fortress Press, 1978), pp. 44-61.
18. Richard Lischer, "The Limits of Story," *Interpretation,* (January 1984), pp. 26-38.
19. Lucy Rose, "Narrative Homiletics: Its Present, Past, and Future," an unpublished essay.
20. Richard Eslinger, *A New Hearing: Living Options in Homiletic Method* (Nashville: Abingdon Press, 1987), pp. 11-14, 65.
21. Hendrikus Berkhof, *Christian Faith* (Grand Rapids: William B. Eerdmans Publishing Company, 1979), p. 357.
22. *Ibid.*, p. 356.
23. Browne, p. 80.
24. *Ibid.*, p. 27.
25. Niebuhr, p. 80.
26. Frederick Buechner, *Telling the Truth* (New York: Harper and Row, 1977), p. 14.
27. William J. Carl III, *Preaching Christian Doctrine* (Philadelphia: Fortress Press, 1984), p. 41.
28. *Ibid.*
29. Keck, p. 107.
30. Gardner C. Taylor, *How Shall They Preach* (Elgin, Illinois: Progressive Baptist Publishing House, 1977), p. 67.
31. Keck, pp. 121-122.
32. *Ibid.*, p. 113.
33. Berkhof, p. 80.
34. Browne, p. 16.

35. Karl Barth, *The Word of God and the Word of Man* (New York: Harper & Brothers, 1957), p. 116.
36. *Ibid.*
37. *Ibid.*, p. 117.
38. Brueggemann, p. 46.
39. *Ibid.*
40. Brueggemann, p. 12.
41. Daniel Day Williams, *The Spirit and the Forms of Love* (New York: Harper & Row, 1968), p. 142.